RAISING ATHLETIC ROYALTY

Insights to Inspire for a Lifetime

Frank Giampaolo

Also Available By Frank Giampaolo

Championship Tennis
(Human Kinetics Worldwide Publishing)

The Tennis Parent's Bible:
A Comprehensive Survival Guide to Becoming a World Class
Tennis Parent (or Coach)

The Mental Emotional Tennis Work Book:
International Player Evaluation

The Mental Emotional Tennis Work Books Series:
Blunders and Cures
Match Chart Collection
Match Day Preparation
How to Attract a College Scholarship

Websites:
http://www.RaisingAthleticRoyalty.com
http://www.MaximizingTennisPotential.com

Printed by CreateSpace

TABLE OF CONTENTS

Mental Toughness
Mistake Management
Lesson: Why Asking Your Kid to Give 110% Is Wrong
Motivation

Negativity
Lesson: Negatron Baton
Nutrition/Hydration
Lesson: Running on Empty

Opportunity
Optimism
Organization
Lesson: Israel Tennis Centers
Overconfidence

Passion
Patience
Parental Over Coaching
Lesson: The Cause of Performance Anxiety
Perfectionism
Lesson: The Fully Developed Human Brain
Perseverance
Persistence
Lesson: What College Coaches Seek
Pessimism
Poise
Positive Outlook
Practice
Preparation
Lesson: The Hobbyist Family
Pressure

ACKNOWLEDGMENTS

To my wife Linda, without her never-ending, loyal attention to detail, this book would have never taken ………....so long.

To Missy DeWalt, for her positive and supportive attitude in helping manage my schedules, websites and social media campaign.

To all the incredible philosophers, educators and motivational writers who've come before. Every attempt has been made to deliver a book of original quotes, phrases and stories. Any similarities are coincidental.

PREFACE

As a veteran teacher, author and parent of a world class athlete, the most common developmental issue I see facing my clients internationally is the inability of gifted athletes to achieve the results they are truly capable of achieving. The question from invested parents is: Why?

The most common answer isn't the athlete's lack of talent; it's the parent's unfamiliarity of the developmental process. It's simply the absence of a modern customized developmental plan. Although parents may have Ivy League degrees or be CEOs of Fortune 500 companies, the skills needed to raise a high-performance athlete are both unique and specific to the athlete and their chosen sport.

In writing **Raising Athletic Royalty**: *Insights to Inspire for a Lifetime*, my goal is to present the information parents and coaches didn't even know… they needed to know. Information such as the importance of the mental and emotional components modern sports psychology/science have identified as essential to elite athletes.

It is the responsibly of the parent of a high-performance athlete to become aware of the 'do's and don'ts' as they manage their child's athletic career. Poor communication (words and actions) can crush the most talented athlete's confidence, destroy enthusiasm and permanently damage the emotional climate great coaches' work to build. Positive communication can increases momentum, reignite commitment and maximize athletic potential.

The evolutionary state of sports demands that parents be more involved. The competition is bigger, faster and stronger than ever before. Around the globe, athletes are training every component of the game with sports science efficiency. Parental influence has the greatest impact on an athlete's success. The words chosen by parents and coaches can make or break a player. It is not just what you say... it is when you say it, your tone of voice, your facial expressions and your body language. Words cause thoughts, thoughts begin action.

To maximize potential at the quickest rate, parents and coaches need to effectively communicate positive modern methodologies throughout the developmental process.

Whether you are motivating a team before practice, driving your child to an athletic event or simply trying to steer your high performance athlete's career, *Raising Athletic Royalty* was written to assist players, parents and coaches in understanding how to encourage, manage and motivate high-performance athletes.

Raising Athletic Royalty is your 'go to guide' to nurturing the greatness found in your children.

INTRODUCTION

Raising Athletic Royalty: *Insights To Inspire for a Lifetime*
presents impactful words, quotes, phrases and illustrative
stories designed to lift the spirits of junior athletes as they
reinforce the positive life lessons athletics affords. The
motivational vocabulary presented in *Raising Athletic Royalty*
will assist parents and coaches in the guidance of their
athletes. Promising players have their best shot at greatness if
they are trained by well-informed parents and coaches.
Choosing the correct, optimistic words at the right time
motivates, inspires, and contributes to the growth of the
player.

Transforming a young junior competitor into athletic royalty
takes more than raw talent and practice. Maximizing athletic
potential does not occur by chance, it takes an organized
plan. This book deciphers the hidden components needed to
rise above the crowd.

It is no accident that certain athletes become great, while the
majority of athletes, some with even more natural talent,
remain average at best. Whatever the sport, the days of raising
a world class athlete by being a passive parent are long gone.
Hobbyist parents raise hobbyist athletes. Experts agree that
the "one size fits all" training methodology is obsolete.

In modern sports science, customizing a developmental plan
begins with understanding the athlete's individual brain and
body type. *Raising Athletic Royalty* goes beyond conventional
means and gently nudges parents into the modern world of
sports psychology. Understanding your child's genetic
proficiencies and deficiencies will help accelerate the learning
curve.

Raising Athletic Royalty will truly enlighten and liberate parents
and coaches with these exciting insights and principles.

MENTAL AND PHYSICAL PREDISPOSITIONS

What if I told you that you think you know your athlete, but you don't? What if I shared a tool to assist you in understanding why your son, daughter or student acts the way they do? What if I showed you why different personalities are better suited for different sports, styles and/or positions? What if I said, to accelerate growth, it is essential that you get into your child's world instead of forcing them into your world? What if I explained how motivating within their genetic guidelines will maximize their potential at a much quicker rate?

"To accelerate growth, it is essential that you get into your child's world instead of forcing them into your world."

The old school teaching/coaching methodology demands the student get into the coach and/or parent's training methodology with total disregard to the student's unique brain and body design. More often than not, this archaic approach produces average athletes at best. At its worst, it quickly causes gifted athletes to leave the game.

Let's begin by recognizing and respecting your child's inborn characteristics. This is commonly known as their brain and body type. Because the most universal personality type indicator is the Myers Briggs Type Indicator (MBTI), I chose to use the MBTI to help you the reader understand athletic profiling. It must be noted that although profiling brain and body types is not a hard science and I am not a neuroscientist or clinical psychologist, I am qualified to maximize athletic potential.

Also worth noting, the founders of the MBTI, Katherine Briggs and Isabel Myers, were not licensed psychologists. They were students passionate about the findings of Carl Jung, the "father" of analytical psychology, and nurtured their love for their chosen field as they designed the now famous MBTI questionnaire.

The MBTI is grouped into four categories with 16 different possible configurations of personality profiles. The four categories list opposing brain types. Each person is assigned a four letter acronym to best describe their primary tendencies. While each of us exhibits multiple sides of our personality, we possess a genetically dominant trait. For example, we all exhibit extraversion and introversion to some degree, but most of us tend to have an overall preference for one over the other.

Listed below are the four MBTI categories with their opposing personality profiles. To help identify your athlete's personality profile, it may be in your best interest to first categorize yourself. Simply read through the four groupings listed below and choose your dominant brain function.

1. **Introvert Versus Extrovert**

Introverts (I) are comfortable lying back then retaliating. They need alone time to recharge their batteries and they prefer to be inside their inner world. **Extroverts** (E) make things happen as they prefer to initiate action. They gain their energy by bringing people together.

2. **Sensate Versus Intuitive**

Sensates (S) prefer to collect data and facts before making their decisions. Facts trump opinions. **Intuitives** (N) trust their gut instincts and are better quick decision makers with 2 seconds left on the clock. They like to "do" first, analyze second.

3. **Thinker Versus Feeler**

Thinkers (T) make decisions through objective logic and impersonalize the situation. They enjoy the technical components and choose truthful over tactful. **Feelers** (F) are in tune with the emotional climate of the event and others actions. Harmony is paramount and they are affected when it is missing.

4.   **Judger Versus Perceiver**

Judgers (J) prefer structure. They like things settled, orderly and precise. They like to make lists to organize their thoughts and prefer to work before play. **Perceivers** (P) are adaptable and flexible. Their thoughts are often found in the future and they enjoy experiencing new ideas and methods versus organizing and agonizing over every boring detail.

Now, write down your four letter acronym. For example, if you believe you're an extrovert, intuitive, feeler, perceivers, then you are an ENFP. Next, Google 'personality profile ENFP' and explore to confirm your assumption. After getting acquainted with the basic personality identification procedure, it is time to brain type your young athlete.

A word of caution: Often certain young people will misdiagnose their own true personality profile as they swap out their true genetic predisposition for what they believe to be a more popular choice.

Now that we have introduced you to brain typing, let me review how body types affect motor skills and athletic potential.

The two opposing body types are called fine motor skilled dominant and gross motor skilled dominant. Individuals have a genetic predisposition to have a motor skill preference. Motor skills are signals sent from the brain through the nervous system into the different muscle groups.

Fine motor skilled athletes excel from the muscles found from the elbows through the hands and fingers. A common compliment given to a fine motor skilled athlete is "They've got good hands."

Gross motor skilled athletes prefer the use of the larger muscle groups found in the torso, legs and feet. Gross motor skilled athletes are known for their superior core balance and elegant body coordination.

Raising athletic royalty requires matching the demands of your child's sport, style of play and/or position with your child's preferred brain type and body type design.

Here is an example of motor skill dominance in American football: a wide receiver's primary job description is to catch the ball. It may prove beneficial if that particular athlete playing that particular position be fine motored skilled dominant (Good hands). However, the field goal kicker in the very same sport, on the very same football team has a very different job description. His primary job is to simply kick the ball. In this athlete's role, it may prove beneficial that his genetic predisposition be gross motor skills dominant (core and leg drive). While it is essential to develop a well-rounded competitor, it's important to note that all athletes possess a dominant body type which naturally excels in their own position and/or sport.

Knowing your child's genetic makeup is critical. It helps to avoid the needless frustrations found in athletic development and in life. Being aware of your athlete's natural strengths and weaknesses will better prepare you to assist and encourage them in their sport, style of play and/or position that they would most naturally excel.

For more detailed information on brain typing, I recommend reading, *Your Key to Sports Success* by Jonathan P. Niednagel.

A

ADVERSITY

LESSON: The Laundry List

"Great game men," said Coach Stevens. "You guys are improving every week. We are one heck of a football team! Every one of you gave it your all out there and I'm so proud! Keep up the good work! I'll see you Tuesday at 4:00 p.m. at Riley Park for practice... READY BREAK!"

Every kid was smiling and laughing walking off the game day field, except for Randy.

Randy knew what was to come. As he slowly headed toward his father's car his stomach was a churning ball of knots. Randy added a limp to his gait to support the ever present fake injury. He placed his cell phone in hand to begin to text his friend about homework the moment he got into the car. These were just a few of the aversion tactics Randy regularly employed to lessen the barrage of criticism that was sure to come from his father. If he pretended to be injured and was addressing the importance of homework he needed to complete, then his father may go easy on him.

You see Randy's dad believed that he was actually helping Randy by watching every game and compiling a detailed laundry list of Randy's failed plays, mistakes and improvement issues. Randy's dad didn't even realize that he was destroying his son's confidence and self-esteem by pointing out his every flaw. No matter how good Randy was, it was not good enough. No matter how long Randy trained, it was not long enough. No matter how many things Randy fixed, his dad would find more flaws.

Mr. Wilson did not have a clue that the only thing he was cultivating was excuses, no effort and zero enjoyment for the sport, not to mention a seriously unhealthy family environment. After all, why in the world would Randy want to play if it only led to a new laundry list of why he's so slow, uncoordinated and stupid?

Parents, remember that the only comments you should make directly after competition are motivational and positive comments like: "I wish I had the guts to go out there and perform like that.", "I think it's so cool watching you out there.", "You're getting better and better everything day.", "Did you have fun out there today?" or "You're playing great; let me know if I can help you with anything!" Motivating the growth you seek comes from optimism and not from pessimism. Continually reminding your children of their failures is futile. Instead, after each game or practice session, support your child's efforts with love and praise.

If you or your spouse possess this dreaded parental laundry list of failure disease, begin to replace the list of negative remarks with positive ones.

If you deeply feel that your laundry list is insightful and important to the growth of your child, I suggest asking the coach if you can email the list to him after the game. Then ask him if he can pay special attention to those issues. Chances are that your child will accept the valid feedback if it is presented by the coach instead of the parent. A good coach should have a better way of presenting the issues in an optimistic and positive light.

"The parental role should be one of gratitude and optimism versus stress and pessimism."

"RECOGNIZE THAT ATHLETIC DEVELOPMENT IS OFTEN THREE STEPS FORWARD & TWO STEPS BACK."

"Under game day adversity, champions choose to stay on script. This is performing in the manner in which they have been trained."

"You and your child may not realize it at the time, but adversity motivates improvement."

"The ability to handle adversity is a learned behavior. Simulate times of controversy in practice and rehearse how your child should handle it."

ANGER

"PLAYING ANGRY ALMOST ALWAYS GUARANTEES FOUR UNPLEASANTRIES: LACK OF A GAME PLAN, THE INABILITY TO STAY IN THE MOMENT, INEFFICIENT MOTOR PROGRAMS, AND THAT YOU WILL LOSE AT A FASTER RATE."

"Playing angry is a sign of being underprepared for competition."

"To stop performing angrily, boldly do what the moment demands and let go of the outcome."

"If your child has trouble accepting that they have anger management issues, review the following steps. Step one is admitting that anger is affecting their performance. Step two is taking the time to organize an action plan to fix the issues. Step three is rehearsing the pre-set protocols until they are wired. Without acceptance, there is no recovery."

"Performing with anger is a phase champions briefly pass through and the average athlete chooses to hang on to..."

ASSESSMENT

LESSON: **Customizing a Developmental Plan**

When I accept a new client, I begin their session with a collection of detailed information as part of my Customized Evaluation Package. Upon completion of the evaluation, each component of the athlete's game is systematically graded by three separate entities: the player, the parent and I. Most often, three different opinions result. Typically, the players think they are great in all categories regardless of their actual skill level, the typical Type A personality parents believe their children are underachieving in most categories and I represent an unbiased professional opinion (usually somewhere in the middle). My role is to find a synergy of energy to bridge the gap between parent and child so a harmonious organizational plan can be activated to maximize potential.

I begin by gaining an understanding of the child's personality profile, their athleticism, their athletic history, as well as their family's athletic history. We don't stop there. Discussions cover their general sports IQ (intelligence quotient), their current weekly developmental schedule, their academic schedule, their social calendars and their sport specific schedules. We then dive into their sport specific IQ, their current technical skills, their opinions regarding the demands of physical fitness, mental tenacity, and their emotional skill sets. All assets and liabilities are assessed before a customized developmental plan is put into effect.

This organizational process of designing an athletic blue-print should be the parent's primary responsibility but is most often left to chance. Parents who take the time to develop a customized plan put their child in a position to maximize their potential at a faster rate. Note that for each stage of adolescence (early/mid/late), there are several common developmental protocols that most coaches follow. I challenge you to go deeper.

"ASSESSING YOUR CHILD'S ABILITIES AND DEVELOPING A CUSTOMIZED GAME PLAN BEGINS WITH UNDERSTANDING THEIR INBORN STRENGTHS AND WEAKNESSES. THEIR BRAIN TYPE AND BODY TYPE PLAY THE MOST IMPORTANT ROLE IN UNDERSTANDING THEIR DEVELOPMENTAL PATHWAY."

"Assessing requires you to study the important components found in your child's sport and list their actual skill level in each. The basic four assessment areas are technical, physical fitness, mental and emotional."

"Athletic self-assessment is often as unreliable as self-personality profiling. Reality is often suppressed to allow dreams and wishes to take center stage."

"Post-performance logs/journals are assessments that expose the actual weaknesses that need to be improved upon and strengths that need to be recognized. Athletes neglecting to review performances will not maximize potential."

"IMPROVEMENT BEGINS WITH DISTINGUISHING MEANINGFUL ACTIVITIES THAT NURTURE GROWTH FROM MEANINGLESS ACTIVITIES THAT SLOW GROWTH AND WASTE TIME. LIST TIME WASTERS AND SYSTEMATICALLY CUT THEM OUT."

ATTITUDE

"ATTITUDE IMPACTS LIFE MORE THAN TALENT, EDUCATION, AND MONEY."

"A positive 'can do' attitude precedes all great performances."

"YOU OFTEN LEARN MORE FROM SCARS THAN DEGREES."

"Positive and negative attitudes and outlooks are daily choices and are extremely contagious."

"Don't focus on the need to always win. Focus on the need to always improve."

"Developing a positive attitude is a lifelong choice."

B

BATTLES

LESSON: **Battling is Optional**

I got a call from Jim Thompson from Columbus, Ohio. "My son is one of the most talented athletes out there, but he can't do anything right under pressure." After an hour on the phone, Jim decided to book a Delta flight to Southern California for him and his son Jordon for a 2-day session.

After I asked a series of brief introductory questions, we discussed how maximizing potential begins when a parent or coach stops forcing the athlete into their way of thinking and enters into the child's world. After a few minutes, it was clear that Mr. Thompson's ISTJ personality profile was polar opposite to Jordan's ENFP profile. Not only did Jordan see the world differently than his father, he had a contrasting style of completing tasks and was wired with a very different set of proficiencies and deficiencies. Jim went from answering most questions that I asked Jordan to becoming silent.

Jim began to realize how differently he and son viewed the world. With tears in his eyes, Jim said "I've been raising my son wrong for the last 14 years! I seriously believed that my way of thinking was the only way, without regard to Jordan's personality preference. I have been stunting his growth. Jordan, I'm so sorry." As he apologized to Jordan, they both began to cry.

Jordan told me during a Skype session a few weeks later that the experience changed their entire family chemistry. He said "My dad now tells me he loves me. He never did that before." Understanding personality profiles has been known to bring harmony to an otherwise chaotic environment.

"UNDERSTANDING PERSONALITY PROFILING WILL HELP YOU AVOID A LARGE PERCENTAGE OF YOUR BATTLES."

"Choose your battles wisely. Understand that when to battle is as important as what to battle."

"Choosing what battles are negotiable and which are non-negotiable is based on your moral code."

"PARENTS, DURING A BATTLE WITH YOUR CHILD, ENCOURAGE SOLUTIONS VERSUS SIMPLY LISTING PROBLEMS."

"If you need to control everyone and everything, you'll lose in the long run. Raising athletic royalty is a compromise."

"Harmony is found when families take the time to look into how each individual is wired and respect how this may affect what they say or what they do."

BELIEF

"Once the parent and the player are mature enough to let go of the outcome of competition (winning or losing), the player is then free to focus on preparing and performing to the best of their ability (peak level)."

"Teach belief even more than technique."

"YOUR PLAYER WILL BELIEVE WHAT YOU PREACH- BOTH POSITIVE AND NEGATIVE. IF YOU ARE ALWAYS SHARING WHAT'S WRONG, YOUR PLAYER WILL DEEPLY BELIEVE THAT THEY'RE ALWAYS.... WRONG."

"Belief comes from success. Always playing your child up may get them comfortable losing."

"The most important life skill to foster every day is belief."

"Believe in working harder, smarter and the confidence will ensue."

BODY LANGUAGE

"Intimidation is a major component in sports. Whether you are the parent or the athlete, control your body language and facial expressions because they reveal your thoughts and emotions."

"Parents, teach your athlete to role play confidence until the act is so comfortable, it becomes real."

"POSITIVE POSTURE AND PRESENCE SERVE TWO IMPORTANT PURPOSES: THEY INFLATE YOUR ENERGY AND DEFLATE YOUR OPPONENT'S ENERGY."

"Projecting negative emotions is a precursor to a bad performance."

BOUNDARIES

"PARENTS NEED TO SET BOUNDARIES. THESE ARE THE LINES OF RESPONSIBILITY. DOING EVERY LITTLE THING FOR YOUR CHILD STUNTS THE GROWTH YOU SEEK. MATURE ATHLETES ARE PROBLEM SOLVERS.

PROBLEM SOLVING IS A LEARNED SKILL THAT IS ESSENTIAL AT THE HIGHER LEVELS OF ALL SPORTS."

"Junior athletes learn from the consequences of their destructive behaviors. They need to experience the occasional failures caused by their own doing to maximize potential."

"Set boundaries between your outside relationships (work, friends and their stresses) and your child's sports relationship. Often a parent's attitude after a bad day at the office trickles down into a toxic relationship with their child during practice."

"Intermediate level players often have a difficult time setting boundaries with their normal friends or siblings who consistently try to pull them away from their goals."

"TEACH YOUR CHILD TO HAVE PERSONAL BOUNDARIES SUCH AS: I WILL NOT ALLOW ANYONE TO ABUSE ME PHYSICALLY, MENTALLY OR EMOTIONALLY. I WILL NOT ALLOW PEOPLE TO LIE TO ME, CHEAT ME OR STEAL FROM ME. I WILL NOT BE PULLED INTO A NEGATIVE WAY OF THINKING OR A PESSIMISTIC ENVIRONMENT."

BRAIN TYPING

"KNOWING YOUR CHILD'S BRAIN TYPE EXPOSES THEIR INBORN, NATURAL PROFICIENCIES AND DEFICIENCIES. THIS ALONE GREATLY INCREASES THE LEARNING CURVE."

"Understanding why people say what they say, think how they think and do what they do is a largely a function of their inborn code."

"EDUCATING YOUR CHILD ABOUT DIFFERENT INBORN PERSONALITIES TRAITS HELPS THEM NAVIGATE RELATIONSHIPS WITH SIBLINGS, TEAMMATES, COACHES AND TEACHERS."

"Knowing your child's brain type will assist you in guiding them through their athletic developmental pathway. It aids in discovering their best sports, style of play or position."

"Recognizing your child's brain and body type will assist you in steering them towards the hobbies, musical instrument, and academic pathway that coincides with their inborn talents and interests."

29

"LEARNING ABOUT BRAIN TYPES WILL AID THEM IN UNDERSTANDING HOW DIFFERENT PEOPLE 'TICK' THIS BENEFITS THEIR LIFE LONG LEADERSHIP SKILLS."

"Mastering brain typing brings harmony to every relationship because it helps you recognize that opposing views are not personal insults; they are simply a function of a person's genetic makeup. Different personality profiles see things from a different perspective."

"MOST IMPORTANTLY, UNDERSTANDING THEIR OWN PERSONALITY PROFILE ASSISTS THEM IN CHOOSING A MEANINGFUL CAREER PATH THAT THEY NATURALLY ALIGN AND EXCEL."

BURNOUT

"Intelligent parents demand rest and recovery. An athlete has to rebuild the body and spirit each week."

"Rest and relaxation are two critical components to long term success."

"Burnout often comes from extended stress and pressure from the entourage."

"THERE ARE DIFFERENT FORMS OF EXHAUSTION WHICH LEAD TO BURNOUT- PHYSICAL, MENTAL AND EMOTIONAL."

"Everyone's stress/pain tolerance levels are different."

"SCHEDULE 'DE-STRESSING' ACTIVITIES IN YOUR PLAYER'S SCHEDULE THAT ARE UNLIKE YOU CHILD'S SPORT TO HELP THEM DECOMPRESS."

"Allow your child to customize their 'own' de-stressing activities."

C

CHALLENGES

"DON'T MAKE YOUR UNWILLINGNESS TO CHANGE BE ONE OF YOUR CHALLENGES. GROWTH COMES FROM CHANGE."

"While weight training strengthens physical muscle, overcoming difficulties and hardships strengthen the head and heart."

"REMEMBER, IT TAKES APPROXIMATELY 4-6 WEEKS TO CHANGE A MOTOR PROGRAM. ASKING YOUR CHILD TO CHANGE A FLAWED ROUTINE RIGHT BEFORE COMPETITION IS A RECIPE FOR DISASTER."

"Overcoming technical, mental or emotional challenges often requires trimming the fat -Doing less is doing more."

CHANGE

"To improve you must embrace change. The game is ever evolving. Refusing to stay current may lead to stagnation."

"NOT BEING ABLE TO APPLY THE SOLUTION TO A NEW PROBLEM OFTEN COMES FROM THE NEED TO HOLD ONTO THE OLD COMFORTABLE, FLAWED WAYS OF ACTING AND THINKING."

"POSITIVE CHANGE REQUIRES YOU TO UNDERSTAND THAT IT USUALLY GETS WORSE BEFORE IT GETS BETTER."

"Terminal intermediates resist change, insisting their way is good enough. Champions welcome change, as a pathway to improvement."

"IF YOU DEEPLY FEEL YOU'RE CAPABLE OF GREATER RESULTS BUT ARE TOO STUBBORN TO CHANGE YOUR DEVELOPMENTAL PLAN...YOU'LL MOST LIKELY KEEP GETTING POOR RESULTS."

"BE WILLING TO TRADE IN 'GOOD ENOUGH' FOR GREAT. GOOD IS FOUND IN EVERY NEIGHBORHOOD."

"Stubborn juniors often waste 45 minutes of their one hour private lesson forcing the professional to continually 'sell' the benefits of fixing the flaw which leaves about 10 minutes to fix it."

"IN LIFE, YOU HAVE TO RISK LOSING IT TO CHANGE IT... AND CHANGE IT TO IMPROVE IT."

CHARACTER BUILDING

"CHAMPIONS TRAIN LIKE CHAMPIONS YEARS BEFORE THEY ACTUALLY BECOME A CHAMPION."

"Your reputation and character precedes you wherever you go."

"Positive character building is a family choice."

"ATTITUDE DETERMINES CHARACTER. YOU CAN CHOOSE TO SWITCH EVERY NEGATIVE THOUGHT AND ACTION TO A POSITIVE ONE."

"Strength of character appears during adversity."

"IN TRAINING, YOU MUST LEARN TO BE COMFORTABLE BEING UNCOMFORTABLE BECAUSE COMPETITION IS UNCOMFORTABLE."

"You must leave your comfort zone to build character."

"STRONG CHARACTER COMES FROM CHOOSING TO LEARN FROM EVERY SETBACK."

"Applying gamesmanship, outside of the rules, is a coward's approach. Applying gamesmanship inside the rules is a champion's approach."

"COMPLIMENT YOUR OPPONENTS AFTER THE GAME INSTEAD OF CRITICIZING THEM ON THE DRIVE HOME."

"Parents, you can't develop a high level athlete by constantly tearing them down."

CHOICES

"Parents compare your child's performance against their peak performance level in practice instead of comparing your child's performance against other children's performances."

"Choose a path: don't play at all, play as a hobbyist, or commit to excellence and train and play as a champion."

"IF THERE WAS ONE THING TO CHANGE WHILE DEVELOPING A YOUNG ATHLETE IT WOULD BE TO CHANGE THE WHAT IF I FAIL MENTALITY TO WHAT IF I CAN'T FAIL."

"CHOOSE TO SEE THE OPPORTUNITIES FOUND IN CONQUERING DIFFICULTIES INSTEAD OF LISTING THE DIFFICULTIES FOUND IN EACH OPPORTUNITY."

"Juniors who live an average athletic life still let the fear of failure stop them. Juniors who have earned their

*athletic royalty status have chosen to not allow their fear
of failure to get in their way."*

COMMITMENT

LESSON: **Junior Failures or Parental Failures?**

Mrs. Azoula brought her 13-year-old daughter Erin down
from Los Angeles for an evaluation. She and her husband
shared an interesting opinion regarding sports development.
They believed Erin should be doing everything for herself,
because it was her dream. They would pay for one private
lesson a week and the rest was up to Erin. They then became
very frustrated when Erin began falling drastically behind the
rest of the junior high players.

As our session got under way, we discussed the job
description of the parents of athletic royalty. Mrs. Azoula was
quick to realize that her daughter's failures were actually
parental failures.

Developing a NCAA D-1 athlete takes the full time
commitment of a primary parent to manage the entourage of
coaches, trainers, schedules, equipment, practice partners and
logistics. No child becomes top in their field without help.
Worldly examples include: Tiger Woods, Wayne Gretzky,
Maria Sharapova, Michelangelo, Mozart, Michael Jackson,
Bruno Mars, Rory McIlroy, Taylor Swift and Andre Agassi.
The secret behind most phenoms is a full-time parental
figure. High-performance success requires a developmental
plan managed by a primary parent and/or a hired expert.

"Commit to the fact that practice doesn't always make perfect, but deliberate customized practice makes excellence."

"Commit to deliberate customized training and results will follow."

"TRAIN PROPERLY EVEN WHEN NO ONE IS WATCHING."

COMMUNICATION

"LISTENING IS THE MISSING LINK TO COMMUNICATION AND HARMONY."

"Pre-game communication should center on probable game scenarios and the correct protocols versus the need to win and the opponent's past results."

"PARENTS, BE AWARE THAT CHILDREN ARE MORE IN TUNE TO YOUR ACTIONS THAN YOUR WORDS."

"FOCUS YOUR COMMUNICATION ON CONTROLLING THE CONTROLLABLE ISSUES VERSUS BANTERING ABOUT THE IRRELEVANT, UNCONTROLLABLE ISSUES."

"DON'T EXPECT YOUR CHILD TO BELIEVE IN THEIR STRENGTHS, IF ALL YOU EVER TALK ABOUT IS THEIR WEAKNESSES."

CONCENTRATION

"Concentration is staying in the moment. Staying in the moment leads to recognizing appropriate plays and patterns, opponent profiling and millisecond anticipation."

"BOTH DEPTH AND LENGTH OF CONCENTRATION ARE REQUIRED AT THE HIGHER LEVELS."

"You can't react and execute properly if your head is not in the moment."

"Concentration is a mental, emotional skill that takes actual practice, focus and discipline."

"ELIMINATING INTERNAL AND EXTERNAL DISTRACTION IS AN ONGOING PROCESS WITHIN THE ART OF CONCENTRATION."

"A lack of concentration may stem from a wandering mind. Your mind follows your eyes."

"Keep your eyes and thoughts inside the lines during competition."

"FOCUS ON ONLY EXECUTING EXACTLY WHAT THE MOMENT DEMANDS."

"IN EVERY SPORT, PEAK PERFORMANCE IS DEPENDENT ON THE ABILITY TO CALM INTENSITY AND IGNITE INTENSITY AT THE APPROPRIATE MOMENT."

CONFIDENCE

"CONFIDENCE IS A PRODUCT OF DEPENDABILITY."

"Confidence allows you to trust yourself and your training."

"Don't expect your child to play with confidence if you're allowing them to train improperly."

"CONFIDENCE IS EARNED THROUGH PROPER PREPARATION. IT PRECEDES SUCCESS."

"Nothing breeds confidence like winning. Success is contagious."

"AN OPTIMISTIC, POSITIVE OUTLOOK FOSTERS ENJOYMENT AND CONFIDENCE; A PESSIMISTIC, NEGATIVE OUTLOOK FOSTERS FEAR AND SELF-DOUBT."

"Fear of failure results from your negative thoughts running the show."

CONSISTENCY

LESSON: **Play the Hits**

There is an interesting parallel between a professional athlete and a professional singer/songwriter. First and foremost, they're both performers. A spark was ignited and that little flame was nurtured into a wild fire.

Singer/songwriters spend thousands of hours writing hundreds of songs throughout their careers and are extremely lucky to have 3-4 hits. These are their go-to money makers. Their label spends millions to get them in rotation on the major radio station across the country. If and when the song charts, the smaller stations jump on board. On the road, the label books the artist at radio stations in each town to play an acoustic version of the hits and promote the release on early morning drive -time stations.

The artist tours most of the year earning millions by featuring the performances of those 3-4 hit songs. The hit songs are the reason why tickets are sold and arenas are filled. A sure fire way to ensure that they lose their beloved audience is by refusing to play their hits and choosing instead to play an hour and a half of reckless obscure cuts. Successful artists know what songs generate their success and showcase them religiously.

Now let's look into the life of a professional tennis player. They too develop their skills for thousands of hours. Their passion for the game (spark) is nurtured into a career (flame.) They have 3-4 off the chart weapons (hits) and these weapons help them win.

Their parents and/or government funded developmental program spends hundreds of thousands of dollars developing the skills and positioning them into ITF (International Tennis

Federation) and then semi-pro events around the world for years on end.

The athlete, like the singer, simply runs his same old boring 3-4 great weapons in the form of patterns every week. It doesn't matter if it's in Miami or Moscow, on grass, clay or hard courts, in the first round or the finals. These pro athletes run their greatest hits day in day out just like the singer/songwriters. This is the reason why tickets are sold and tennis arenas are filled.

A sure fire way for a professional tennis player to ensure that he/she loses the audiences' admiration (not to mention, loss of consistency and success) would be by going for obscure, reckless shot selections.

It would be wise for most junior athletes to know their strengths and nurture their weapons until they're devastating great. In today's sports, you have to possess "hits." Once developed, an intelligent athlete consistently applies those weapons at crunch time.

Whether you're a singer or an athlete, plan on developing your secret weapons and play those greatest hits all the way to the bank for as long as possible.

"CONSISTENCY STARTS WITH CONSISTENT THOUGHTS WHICH THEN OPEN THE DOORS TO CONSISTENT MOTIVATION, PREPARATION AND TRAINING REGIMENS, WHICH THEN LEADS TO CONSISTENT PERFORMANCES."

"Parents, please try to remain emotionally consistent after wins and losses. Your bitterness after a loss is the anchor sinking future performances."

"CONSISTENT GAME PERFORMANCE BEGINS WITH REPLICATING GAME DAY STRESSORS IN THE PRACTICE SESSIONS."

"REPETITION IS THE GODFATHER OF CONSISTENCY."

"PRACTICE IN THE MANNER YOU'RE EXPECTED TO PERFORM AND THEN PERFORM IN THE MANNER YOU'VE BEEN TRAINING."

"Consistently develop the technical, mental, emotional and physical skill sets of your chosen sport. Each component is mandatory in the higher levels."

"HAVING THE 'POTENTIAL' IS A LABEL YOU GET UNTIL YOU BEGIN TO APPLY DELIBERATE CUSTOMIZED TRAINING ON A CONSISTENT BASIS."

"Athletic royalty is a result of consistent success."

CONTROL THE CONTROLLABLES

"FOCUS ON WHAT IS IN YOUR CONTROL: SUCH AS YOUR ATTITUDE, FIGHT, WORK ETHIC, CONCENTRATION, PERFORMANCE GOALS AND RITUALS."

"Let go of worrying about uncontrollables such as the weather, start times, rankings, who's watching, the draw, and what others may or may not be thinking."

"PERFORMANCE GOALS ARE USUALLY FOUND BY STAYING IN THE PRESENT. OUTCOME GOALS CREEP IN WHEN YOUR THOUGHTS SLIP INTO THE PAST OR FUTURE."

"ATHLETES ARE ACTORS. WHEN IT'S TIME TO WORK, THE GREAT ONES LEAVE THEIR OWN WORLD AND SHIFT INTO CHARACTER."

"Parents and players, if you have a deep need to control, focus on self-control. Control your discipline, your effort, your attitude and your perseverance versus trying to control everyone else."

"IDENTIFY AND CONTROL THE INNER BATTLES...THE ONES FOUGHT BETWEEN THE EARS."

COURAGE

"To shut out the demons on your shoulder requires effort, focus and courage."

"Parents, courage is contagious: promote it, encourage it and live it!"

"RISK GOING TOO FAR AND YOU JUST MIGHT CREATE A BETTER YOU."

"Courage is trusting and applying your developmental plan under pressure."

"DON'T JUST DARE TO DREAM, HAVE THE COURAGE TO CHASE THAT DREAM."

"FUTURE CHAMPIONS HAVE THE INSIGHT AND COURAGE TO EXCEED THE CURRENT STANDARDS OF TRAINING."

"Courage, desire, and the competitive fire are sometimes inborn but most often need to be nurtured."

"COURAGE IS FORGETTING FEAR FOR A FEW HOURS."

"Realize that your competitors are most likely a few heartbeats away from cracking. They will crack ...if you don't."

CRITICISM

LESSON: **Reverse Psychology**

Finally, I've got a day off. I'm home in Laguna. It's another perfect, sunny Thursday morning. I decided to throw my golf clubs into the trunk and spend an hour on the tranquil driving range in San Juan Capistrano. A morning at the range wouldn't be complete without a quick stop at Los Golandrinos for their killer breakfast burrito. Potatoes, ham, eggs, cheese and their crazy hot salsa seem to help my horrible golf game.

After the last bite, I drive down PCH with the top down to the club. As I purchase the large bucket of balls and drop my clubs by an open range slot I overheard them... "COME ON JOEY! ...You're still lifting your head before contact. How many times do I have to remind you! KEEP YOUR HEAD DOWN UNTIL THE STINKIN BALL IS GONE!" barks the older gentleman. Right on cue, Joey throws his 7 iron to the ground, shakes his head and yells, "SHUT UP DAD! I can't concentrate when you keep talking! I'm not an idiot ... I know! The more you tell me, the more I can't do it!"

This bantering went on for about 20 more minutes. Every time it got a little too peaceful, I hear "Same thing Joe! Jesus…You're still pulling out! Come on FOCUS! ...HEAD DOWN!!" his dad complained.

Frustrated, the dad walks away, past me towards the snack shop. Knowing that I'll get no peace with this bantering father -son sideshow; I decide to offer some advice.

I get in line behind the dad and introduce myself. I mention that I work with high-performance athletes around the world and can I offer a practical tip that just may help Joey? "Sure, I'll take anything that'll get him to listen," says the dad. I said, "Instead of continuing to tell him that he's still doing it wrong, reverse it." He gives me a weird look.

I told him to trust me and go back to the range, watch a few swings, and then flip your energy, attitude and advice. Say… Nice Joey! You're getting it! You kept your head down through the strike zone! Even, if he isn't actually doing it correctly. He will then relax and actually turn his negative "I can't do it" attitude into a positive 'I can do it' attitude. Not only will he focus on fixing his own technical flaw, but more importantly you will be allowing him to keep his ego and integrity. I explained that it was reverse psychology…and worth a try. He smiled as he thanked me and agreed to give it shot.

The energy on that side of the driving range flipped from a pessimistic toxic environment to an optimistic environment. Anger turned to laughter as Joey relaxed, de-stressed and began to hit straight and long.

If someone was constantly pestering and belittling you about your faults, would it annoy you? Of course, it would.

If your child is a natural born negotiator here is another reverse psychology trick. If you feel it's beneficial for her to do 25 push-ups, ask her to do 50. She'll negotiate down to 25. You'll smile inward as you agree to let her win the negotiation.

"It's amazing what your child will do if you know how to avoid the negative confrontations and apply a bit of optimistic encouragement."

"REVERSE PSYCHOLOGY WORKS WONDERS. INSTEAD OF SAYING, '_____IS STILL WRONG', SAY 'YOU'RE REALLY STARTING TO DO _____ SO MUCH BETTER'. YOU'LL GET THE RESULTS AND ALLOW YOUR CHILD TO KEEP THEIR INTEGRITY AND SELF-CONFIDENCE."

"Parents, for every one negative comment deliver five positive comments. Children usually only hear the negative comment and ignore the positive comments."

"CONSTRUCTIVE CRITICISM ISN'T REALLY SEEN AS CONSTRUCTIVE. KIDS SEE IT AS SUGAR COATED BLAME."

"Frame criticism as opportunities for improvement and not as a personal insult."

"PARENTS, REMEMBER DISTANCE BRINGS CLARITY. THE WORST TIME TO CRITIQUE YOUR CHILD'S PERFORMANCE IS IMMEDIATELY AFTER A TOUGH LOSS."

"Celebrate the strength and integrity of your child. They have to put their reputation on the line week in and week out competing and developing."

"GIVE THE MOST STRESSFUL PARENT THE INSIDE JOBS OF LOGISTICS MANAGER, EQUIPMENT MANAGER, AND SCHEDULING MANAGER. BEFORE LEAVING FOR THE COMPETITION, KISS THEM GOODBYE AS YOU LEAVE THEM AT HOME."

D

DEDICATION

"DEDICATING ONE'S SELF TO A SPORT IS A LIFESTYLE CHOICE. CHAMPIONS ARE NOT PART TIME HOBBYISTS."

"Apply the school methodology to dedicated training. Just as school children attend a variety of classes daily, athletes should train a variety of customized components daily."

"Being dedicated to your sport requires taking the 20 hours a week you spend on Facebook, Twitter and Instagram and devote that time to training instead."

"DEDICATE YOURSELF TO DELIBERATE CUSTOMIZED TRAINING VERSUS RELYING SOLELY ON GROUP TRAINING."

"Your athlete gets 168 hours each week. Deduct the hours spent for sleep, school, homework and meals. Training to become athletic royalty requires approximately 20 hours a week. Does your athlete have the time?"

DISCIPLINE

*"DISCIPLINE GETS YOU WHAT YOU WORK FOR...
WHICH THEN LEADS YOU TO GETTING WHAT YOU
HOPE FOR..."*

*"Discipline is part of your child's moral code. It's an
essential building block for greatness."*

*"A disciplined athlete often wins even when they are
playing less than 100% of their norm."*

*"A DISCIPLINED PLAYER WITH AVERAGE ATHLETIC
ABILITY SOON TRUMPS A SUPERB ATHLETE WITH NO
DISCIPLINE."*

*"Great coaches and parents teach the art of self-
discipline and accountability."*

*"SELF-DISCIPLINED ATHLETES ARE AT THE TOP OF
THE LIST WHEN IT COMES TO THE COLLEGE
RECRUITING PROCESS."*

"Role models, over-achievers and athletic royalty all have been nurtured in the art of self-discipline."

E

EFFORT

LESSON: **You Must Be Present To Win**

Steve was a talented junior tennis player who started to play on the national scene later than most. Due to the ranking system, he didn't qualify for the prestigious Easter Bowl Super National Tennis Tournament. During his training session, I discussed with his mother that Steve was only 7 spots out and 5 of the other players listed above him weren't from California. They were unlikely to fly to Palm Springs if they were still on the alternate list.

My motivational pitch was, "You have to be present to win." Make the effort and drive to Palm Springs. It's only a 2 1/2 hour drive. If he gets into the event, great! If not, spend the day together watching the top seeds play, hiking the mountains, visiting the Cabazon outlet mall and enjoying your time together.

After a few days of trying to convince her, Ellen finally agreed to drive to Palm Springs, even though she had to remind me how she hated to waste the weekend. They decided to make the effort and take the chance.

I said, "Great. Just make sure that from now until the event, he trains daily like he is 100% in the draw."

Well, Steve not only got into the event at the last hour but got a great draw. He went on to win 4 rounds losing in the semifinals. Steve's national ranking shot up into the USTA (United States Tennis Association) top 50. He never again had to qualify for a national. He was even seeded in future, lower level national events. Due to his new found high ranking, Steve was offered a terrific full ride scholarship to one of his favorite NCAA colleges and today enjoys his athletic royalty status. You must be present to win.

"Effort unlocks each child's hidden potential."

"EFFORT STEMS FROM ATTITUDE."

"PARENTS, REMEMBER TO PLACE TREMENDOUS EFFORT IN THE ENJOYMENT OF THE JOURNEY AND THE GRATIFICATION OF THE CHASE."

"Effort is the foundation of growth and growth creates results."

"Continuous, focused effort transforms a normal local kid into a national champion."

"RECOGNIZE EFFORT, PRAISE EFFORT, APPRECIATE EFFORT, INSPIRE EFFORT, GIVE KUDOS TO EFFORT, COMPLIMENT EFFORT, DEMAND EFFORT, AND CELEBRATE YOUR ATHLETE'S EFFORT."

"EFFORT IS A CHOICE."

"Make it your mission to make effort your brand name."

"EFFORT IS MAKING EACH PRACTICE SESSION EPIC."

EGO

"Parents, congratulations, you played sports in high school or college back in the day. Now, relinquish the need to control practice sessions and teach those old school, obsolete methods to your child."

"Don't let your ego as a coach or parent stand in the way of your child's success."

"WHEN HIRING COACHES USE THIS ANALOGY: WHEN BUILDING A SPACESHIP, HIRE SUCCESSFUL, EXPERIENCED ROCKET SCIENTISTS VERSUS OUT OF WORK MINOR LEAGUE ASTRONAUTS. JUST BECAUSE A COACH MAY CLAIM THEY WERE A FORMER 'CHAMPION', DOESN'T MEAN THEY HAVE THE SKILLS TO TEACH."

"Excuses are a way of protecting the ego."

"Players and parents, playing the blame game is a way of diverting the attention away from the player's lack of proper training and accountability."

"WHAT KIND OF CRAZY PERSON DOES EVERYTHING WITHIN THEIR POWER TO SUCCEED? THE ANSWER IS WINNERS!"

"Put in the hard work from middle school through high school and enjoy the perks and glory of being athletic royalty in College. Dog it now and enjoy paying off your student load until you're old and gray."

EMOTIONAL SKILL SETS

LESSON: **The Replacement Theory**

Zoe is a gifted basketball player. She's wired with great hands. Sports scientists call her body type: fine motor skill dominate. Her father John played NCAA D-3 ball 25 years ago and is her personal coach. He had thrown in the towel on her basketball career because he felt she didn't have what it took. John said, "I point out to her everything that she's doing wrong but she never fixes it!" John demanded Zoe do everything his way, despite the fact that they had opposing personality profiles and body types.

At the eleventh hour, Zoe's mom brought her to see me.

After completing our initial evaluation session it was clear to me that her weakest component was stamina, not just physical, but mental and emotional stamina.

When Zoe got winded, her movement and spacing got sloppy and she went off script with her low percentage shot and passing selections because she was too winded to stay in the moment. More importantly, her emotions went volatile. Zoe confided in me that her parents tell her each day that she has to lose weight. Several coaches told her the same thing. So why didn't she? Unfortunately, she was told the problem multiple times but never the solution to the problem.

After I watched a video clip of her game day performance, we went to the club house. I grabbed two ice teas and we sat on the couch and customized a plan. I helped Zoe understand that she didn't need another coach to teach her fundamentals. She actually needed to replace the outdated training regimens and poor eating habits with a customized developmental plan and new healthy eating habits.

The solution lies in understanding that just saying STOP to most problems simply doesn't work. The key is to replace the bad habits with powerful new good habits.

Zoe proceeded to make a detailed list of everything she ate for the past week. We systematically swapped those meals and snacks with healthier choices. Within 6 weeks Zoe dropped her initial 20 lbs. Along with that, her new deliberate training cleaned up her flaws and her attitude improved as well. She worked her brand new customized developmental plan weekly. Six months later, Zoe was about 40 lbs. lighter and honored with the teams most improved player award.

This replacement theory works wonders for the emotional components found in high performance sports. Just telling your youngster to stop being negative without replacing the situation with a new positive approach simply doesn't work.

Negatives don't just stop cold turkey because we spot them; negatives must be systematically replaced by positive new habits. Successful athletes are solution oriented and not problem oriented.

"THE CURE USED TO DEFEAT REOCCURRING NEGATIVE THOUGHTS IS TO REPLACE THE NEGATIVE THOUGHTS WITH OPTIMISTIC THOUGHTS. JUST SAYING STOP DOES NOT WORK IN THE LONG RUN."

"Know the enemy... it is usually not the opponents. The 'enemy' usually is the demons lurking inside and/or the lack of appropriate training."

"Your actions at crunch time directly reflect your emotional development or lack thereof..."

"EMOTIONAL TOUGHNESS IS RELATED TO THE ABILITY TO HANDLE ADVERSITY UNDER STRESS."

"Poor emotional control such as mistake management can surely derail technique and fluid movement, as well as cloud judgment. Emotional development is mandatory at the higher levels."

"Emotional control is not allowing poor snippets of play to ruin the whole game/day. Sometimes you have to win ugly."

"HOW YOU CHOOSE TO INTERPRET THE EVENT MAKES ALL THE DIFFERENCE IN THE WORLD."

"TO DEVELOP A WORLD CLASS PERSON, E.I. (EMOTIONAL INTELLIGENCE) IS EVEN MORE IMPORTANT THAN I.Q."

ENTHUSIASM

"IT TAKES THOUSANDS OF HOURS OF HARD WORK TO BECOME A CHAMPION. WITHOUT GREAT ENTHUSIASM, FUN AND LAUGHTER YOU DON'T EVEN HAVE A CHANCE."

"Laughter is a key ingredient to the deliberate customized practice method."

"Hard work without compliments, enthusiasm and fun leads to dull depressing practice sessions and negative results."

"Sometimes enthusiasm has to be created."

"ENTHUSIASTICALLY CONGRATULATE GROWTH VERSUS THE PUSH TO ALWAYS WIN."

"Look for coaches that teach enthusiasm as they secretly sneak in technique."

"IT'S A LAW OF NATURE THAT YOU MUST TEACH OPTIMISM AND ENTHUSIASM IF YOU WANT TO SEE OPTIMISM AND ENTHUSIASM."

"For some children, enthusiasm and passion for a sport seems to be inborn. For other children, it's a learned behavior."

EMOTIONAL CONTROL

"Encourage your child to perform fearlessly while applying their peak performance routines instead of harping about the need to win."

"The peak performance state of mind lies between over arousal and under arousal."

"Each of the different personality profiles has their own competitive comfort zones. What's right for one is not always right for another."

"THE ABILITY TO FOCUS FOR THE DURATION AND COPE WITH ADVERSITY IS EMOTIONAL TOUGHNESS."

"Knowing how and when to pump oneself up or calm oneself down is an essential emotional characteristic champions develop."

"Challenge the demons in your head and they will be silenced. Remember, your inner voice greatly impacts your performance."

"EMOTIONAL TOUGHNESS IS ALL ABOUT NOT ACTING LIKE THE VICTIM UNDER STRESS."

ERRORS

LESSON: **Parental Pre-Game Sabotage**

Jake is a 12-year-old all-star soccer player out of Oklahoma City, Oklahoma. He's got serious skills and should be every coach's dream. Sadly, he'll never make the all-stars, the high school squad or play NCAA ball. His issue is his father. When Jake and his dad get out of their car before the game, the coaches cringe as his teammate's positive attitudes sink like lead balloons.

Mr. Cantanoli, Jakes dad, is stuck in the 1960's old school Drill Sergeant mold. He believes that his high stress level presence is actually needed and is helping. Before each game, age old parental blunders spew out of Mr. Cantanoli's mouth.

"Let's go! We HAVE to win today!"; "Losing isn't an option"; "Hey coach, make em do 20 more push-ups for smiling & laughing!; This isn't a joke!"; "I want a perfect 12-0 season!" ; "No one should score on us!...NO ONE!"; "We don't lose... EVER!"

Within minutes, Jake and his teammates seem totally dazed and confused on the field. They hesitate, make mindless errors, they don't trust their training or their teammates, they are not synchronized, they are so petrified to make an error and get reprimanded by Mr.Cantanoli, that they are frozen with fear.

Why? The answer lies in the sadly uninformed Mr. Cantanoli and his poor advice.

In order to achieve great outcomes, players need to de-stress, relax and only focus on their performance goals. Topics like: the job description of their field positions, seeing the field (broad vision skills), solid dribbling and passing, running the pre-set patterns and the actual plays developed in practice. The players need to focus on their offensive and defensive responsibilities. What they don't need is the irrelevant clutter that Mr. Cantanoli is actually putting in their heads right before the game.

All of the terrific performance goals that the coaches spend weeks to perfect get lost in channel capacity when Mr. Cantanoli pulls the players' thoughts away from their task at hand- which is to only focus on their performance goals.

Jake eventually loses interest in playing soccer because of his father's negative behavior. Unfairly, Jake gets all the blame and is labeled a quitter by his dad. If your child read this story would he/she relate? Parents of today's athletes need to be educated about the proper protocols of sports psychology.

"In most sports, there are two types of errors. Forced and unforced. The trick, of course, is to systematically cut out the unforced."

"SPOTTING ERRORS IS A NICE START. SPOTTING THE CAUSE OF THOSE ERRORS IS EVEN BETTER."

"Causes of errors can be categorized into inefficient technique, poor positioning, inappropriate tactics, and/or sloppy focus."

"ERRORS IN SPORTS REVEAL CHARACTER; FIXING THEM BUILDS CHARACTER."

"STAY AT THE COMPETITION EVEN AFTER A LOSS AND PROFILE YOUR COMPETITORS. LEARN WHY THEY'RE STILL IN THE EVENT AND WHY YOU WERE AN EARLY LOSER."

"Spotting errors is easy. Leaving one's comfort zone to actually fix the flaws takes great character and courage."

"TEACH YOUR CHILDREN TO BE ACCOUNTABLE FOR PROBLEM SOLVING. CHAMPIONS SOLVE THEIR OWN PROBLEMS ON AND OFF THE FIELD."

EXCUSES

"You can manufacture results or excuses…pick one."

"Blaming others who are trying to help you is the coward's way out."

"GOOD PLAYERS BECOME GREAT WHEN A COACH HELPS THEM TO ELIMINATE EXCUSES."

"Focusing on the reasons why you can't succeed, will only make you a 'nobody'."

"WHEN YOU'VE EXHAUSTED ALL OF YOUR EXCUSES, THE HARD WORK BEGINS AND THE NEXT CHAMPION IS BORN."

"Excuses are lies told to avoid the possibility of failure."

"USUALLY THE ONLY THING STANDING BETWEEN YOU AND SOLID RESULTS IS YOUR COMMITMENT TO SEEK SOLUTIONS VERSUS EXCUSES."

EXECUTING GAME PLANS

LESSON: **Consistency is a Weapon**

Maggy is a great example of just how intuitive and organized young people can be. I met her by chance on a flight from Los Angeles to Las Vegas- row 17, seats A and B to be exact. I moved my racket bag so she could get her bowling bag on with two 9 lb. bowling balls into the tiny overhead compartment. Time flew by as we sat together and chatted for the hour long flight.

Maggy lived in Reno, Nevada. The cold weather was something Maggy and her family chose to get out of versus something to play in, so they would go bowling, religiously, at the National Bowling Stadium in Reno. It turns out, Maggy was a national powerhouse. She was a member of the Young Americans Bowling Alliance and the United States Bowling Congress.

The conversation turned to her strategic game plan for performing consistently game after game, day after day, week after week, through this year. Her insight was very, very mature for a 16-year-old.

When I asked about her bowling career, she said "Getting good at a sport is just the beginning. Even good league bowlers can score in the high 200's on occasion, good golfers can play professional level holes and good tennis player can play a lights out sets. But the key to success is to see consistency as your ultimate weapon. My open frames come from being unfocused and not being able to stay emotionally stable after an unlucky 7-10 split. Being able to execute the same old boring strikes for a few hundred frames a week is my goal. If I can execute that consistent game plan, I'll be able to compete with the professionals on the PBA (Professional Bowling Association) in a few years."

With a developmental plan focusing on her performance goal of consistency, I have no doubt that we'll see Maggy executing her game plan as a professional bowler very soon.

"A GREAT GAME PLAN IS TO FOCUS ON ELIMINATING UNFORCED ERRORS. CONSISTENCY IS A POWERFUL WEAPON."

"Players who believe that they don't have to play the proper percentages never reach their true potential."

"Shutting down your opponent's primary game plan forces them to shift to a less comfortable, less successful style of play."

"THE ABILITY TO EXECUTE THE SAME OLD BORING WINNING PLAYS OVER AND OVER AGAIN IS BRILLIANT."

"Knowing how to apply strategy and actually executing it depends greatly on emotional control."

"TO EXECUTE WHAT THE MOMENT DEMANDS SEPARATES THE GOOD FROM THE GREAT."

"Great form without execution makes for a good looking loser."

"OVERTHINKING USUALLY RUINS EXECUTION."

"Focusing exclusively on perfect technical form usually ruins the art of execution under stress."

"BEING SCARED OF MAKING ERRORS OR LOOKING BAD LEADS TO POOR EXECUTION."

F

FAILURE

LESSON: **Undermining**

A few years ago I was a featured speaker at the Australian Open's International Coaches Conference. While attending dinner with some of the attendees, the conversation drifted to the usual topic: "Where should we look to find the next crop of champions? A coach from South Africa offered up, "First place I'd look is an orphanage!" The coaches broke into hysterical laughter. (Note: Orphans don't have parents...get it?)

As I travel around the world working with elite athletes, parents and coaches; I am consistently amazed at the sheer number of organizations that instill a "NO PARENT" policy. Their opinions range from: "Athlete's parents are a nuisance that cause more harm than good." to "Dealing with athlete's parents is a negative experience and a waste of time." to my favorite, "Parents think they can help but they only hurt our process."

My opinion is polar opposite.

In my experience, it is essential to educate the parents. Invested, Type-A, selfless parents deeply want to be involved in their own children's lives and be a part of the team. Telling the primary care givers to butt out isn't in anyone's best interest.

Educated parent have so much to contribute to the team's success. Athletes will maximize their potential at a much faster rate with the unity of the entourage. Scorned parents will ultimately undermine and belittle the coach's efforts. Parents who feel that they're a critical part of their child's success will happily enforce and implement the coach's wishes. Their words and actions will either instill critical trust in the coaches or destroy all trust. Parents hold the ultimate power in the success of their children because they have the most influence- as they should.

Parental modeling is leading by example. A parent 'on the team' demonstrates the essential teamwork needed to maximize potential at the quickest rate. If a parent reinforces the coaches/trainers training regimens, the child is more likely to comply and believe. For example, "Johnny, Coach Stevens emailed and wanted me to remind you to do your upper body routine before school." A parent kicked off the team may demonstrate unhealthy team busting behavior, such as, "Johnny, you lost but it's not your fault. Your coach is an idiot! Maybe we should try the Academy down the street?"

Parents reading this will be best served by respecting the hired coaches and trainers and allow them to manage their respective positions. Allow the coaches to teach the mechanics and strategies of the sport. Allow the trainers to oversee the strength and speed components. Parents, if you want to be involved in the process, here's a great start to your parental job description - with humor injected:

- H R Skills: Interviewing, hiring and firing coaches, trainers, sparring partners…with the enthusiasm of Donald Trump.
- Accounting /Banking Skills: possess an extremely thick check book; and be willing and able to max out their major credit cards.
- Designated Driver: Must be willing to put 100 thousand miles on the family car and enjoy most of your meals behind the wheel.
- Expect Your Child to Occasionally Go "Brain Dead": Be willing and able to accept that your child will occasionally forget everything they were taught during

the last $5000.00 worth of training and blow several events a year.

- Scheduling Manager: World class juggling skills required to organize the ever changing schedules of booking practice times & logistics, hired sparring partners or other junior practice partners, lessons and events.
- Booking Agent: Flexible skills required to book last minute airlines, cars and hotels.
- VIP/24 hour Courier Service: laundry service, equipment replacement service, drug store pharmaceuticals pickup and delivery service, bed time psychology sessions.
- Fashion Coordinator/Personal Shopper: Purchasing only the latest gear, shoes and matching clothes.
- Maintenance Knowledge: General maintenance of equipment and cloth malfunctions such as last minute zipper repairs.
- Parental Intuition: Must have the uncanny ability to become expendable and invisible in a seconds notice and/or appear bright eyed or happy to help 2 minutes later…
- Game Day Performance Review: Must be willing to evaluate a crummy performance then point out fifty positive observations but NEVER share negative feedback without starting WWIII
- Game Day Parental Duties: Assisting the athlete as they systematically morph from a goofy kid into a focused Athletic Warrior.

As you can see, there's plenty of work for everyone. In my opinion, parents should be the coach's greatest partner. A large component in the journey of Raising Athletic Royalty is cultivating the winning team/entourage experience.

"CHAMPIONS ARE CHAMPIONS BECAUSE THEY HAVE LOST MANY TIMES AND LEARNED FROM THEIR LOSSES."

"Most junior competitors fail during competition because they choose not to train properly."

"Failure is choosing not to be coachable."

"FAILURE IS ALLOWING NEGATIVE THOUGHTS TO DESTROY YOUR BELIEF."

"What makes losing so scary is fearing the expectations and negative response of others."

"THE RECIPE FOR DISASTER IS FOCUSING ON TRYING NOT TO FAIL."

"Failure begins by being dishonest, unorganized and giving minimal effort on training days."

"REAL FAILURE IS HAVING SKILLS AND DREAMS, BUT NO WORK ETHIC TO REALIZE THEM."

"Failure comes from inflexibility. In sports, things rarely go as planned."

FATIGUE

"Fatigue is usually caused by worry, stress and fear more than from physical training."

"Exercise increases energy and improves your attitude."

"Lack of fitness destroys even the best game plans."

"For most intermediate athletes, fatigue (mental, emotional or physical) causes defeat more often than the opponent."

"FEELINGS OF FATIGUE DURING COMPETITION LEAD TO IMPROPER TECHNIQUE, INADEQUATE MOVEMENT, POOR DECISION MAKING SKILLS AND COWARDLY EMOTIONAL CONTROL."

"Apply periodization training to ensure that your athlete is starting their competition with fully charged physical, mental and emotional batteries."

FEAR

"ONE OF GROWTH'S GREATEST ENEMIES IS THE FEAR OF A NEW IDEA."

"Success at crunch time comes to those who handle fear and their competitive anxieties."

"The inability to handle one's emotional demons is what keeps thousands of gifted athletes from becoming champions."

"IF YOU FEAR CHANGE AND HARD WORK MORE THAN YOU HATE LOSING, YOU PROBABLY WON'T CHANGE. IF YOU HATE LOSING MORE THAN YOU FEAR CHANGE AND HARD WORK, YOU'VE GOT A REAL SHOT AT BEING A CHAMPION."

"IF YOU MUST LIVE IN FEAR... FEAR BEING AVERAGE."

"Proper preparation and pre-match routines will help to quiet fear and nervousness."

FINANCIAL BURDEN

"Avoid talking about how much the sport is costing you in front of your child. This only adds an unnecessary burden your child must carry into competition."

"THE FINANCIAL OBLIGATION REQUIRED TO RAISE ATHLETIC ROYALTY, IS OFTEN SIMILAR TO THE COST OF YOUR CHILD'S COLLEGE TUITION, BUT THE ADDED BENEFITS ARE PROFOUND!"

"IN THIS DAY AND AGE, A HIGH SAT SCORE, GREAT GPA OR CLASS VALEDICTORIAN DOESN'T GUARANTEE COLLEGE ADMISSION. ATHLETIC ROYALTY IS OFTEN THE 'TIPPING POINT' FOR COLLEGE ACCEPTANCE."

"Is your child playing a sport as an extracurricular activity or is your child a high performance athlete. The financial commitment is related to their level of involvement. It is a family choice."

"Parents- if the financial obligation of your child's sport is too great- consider looking for a sponsor. There are several websites devoted to funding."

FOCUS

"FOCUSING FOR THE DURATION IS A MENTAL/EMOTIONAL SKILL. IT REQUIRES STAYING PLUGGED INTO THE VISION AND IN THE MOMENT UNTIL YOU'RE BACK IN THE LOCKER ROOM."

"For most humans, focusing on only a handful of thoughts is incredibly difficult. Therefore, focusing better requires less thinking... not more."

"THOSE WHO FOCUS ON THEIR LIMITATIONS SELDOM REACH THEIR POTENTIAL. THOSE WHO FOCUS ON THEIR POTENTIAL SURPASS THEIR LIMITS."

"IN COMPETITION, CHAMPIONS HAVE A HANDFUL OF THOUGHTS IN THEIR HEADS. INTERMEDIATE ATHLETES HAVE A LAUNDRY LIST OF INAPPROPRIATE THOUGHTS IN THEIR HEADS."

"There are long and short term goals. Great athletes stay focused on both of their lists."

"AVERAGE PARENTS AND COACHES FOCUS ON THE PROBLEMS. GREAT ONES FOCUS ON THE SOLUTIONS."

"Both internal and external distractions need to be acknowledged and eliminated."

"DURING COMPETITION, COMPLACENCY, BOREDOM AND THE INABILITY TO REMAIN IN THE MOMENT ARE THE CAUSE OF A LARGE MAJORITY OF ONE'S LOSSES."

"Eye tracking studies have found good athletes watch the ball, but expert athletes watch the ball AND anticipate the future action/location of teammates and opponents. Anticipatory skills are learned behaviors in high level sports."

FUNDAMENTALS

"FUNDAMENTALS WILL NEVER TRULY BE TAMED BECAUSE THE GAME IS ALWAYS EVOLVING."

"SOLID FUNDAMENTALS GET YOU INTO THE GAME, PHYSICAL FITNESS TAKES YOU DEEPER, BUT IT'S THE

DEVELOPMENT OF THE HIDDEN MENTAL AND
EMOTIONAL SKILLS THAT TAKES YOU OVER THE TOP."

"*Fundamentals in sports are similar to the foundation of
a sky scraper- essential to stability but worthless without
the development of the rest of the building.*"

"REPETITION ISN'T ALWAYS GOOD. GROOVING POOR
FUNDAMENTALS DEVELOPS UNRELIABLE TECHNIQUE
AND CAUSES INJURIES."

"MOST PEOPLE BELIEVE THAT CORRECTING AND
DEVELOPING REQUIRES ADDING MORE. IMPROVING
USUALLY INVOLVES 'TRIMMING THE FAT'. CLEANER
FUNDAMENTALS INCREASE THEIR DEPENDABILITY."

G

GOAL SETTING

LESSON: **You Get What You Pay For**

Dr. Chang Lee practices medicine in Los Angeles. His son Ken enjoys the game of golf and is on the local high school golf team. Ken is a junior and again missed the cut for varsity; he was sent back to the JV squad for another year. Ken wants to play golf for a major university and is seeing his dreams slip away.

Dr. Lee and Ken made the drive down to Laguna to do our three-hour Customized Evaluation Session. After the cordial chatting, we get into the details of Raising Athletic Royalty. Within 15 minutes a reoccurring theme starts to appear. Dr. Lee has Ken in a golf clinic two days a week at his country club. The one-hour clinics consist of 18 junior golfers ranging from the age of 9-17.

The clinic is marketed to be taught by the club's golf director, an X-PGA player, but it is really run by his two assistant pros. In reality, Ken gets access to the range and a 9-1 ratio of player to pro for two hours a week.

I explained that range hitting isn't "practicing in the manner in which you're expected to perform." It's simply block learning being applied in a game that requires very different flexible skill sets. The type of grass, length of grass, slope of the lie and the weather are just a few variables that must be addressed in the game of golf. Managing performance pressure, club selection, focus control and reading the course all play a part in Ken's ability to shoot a low score. Besides, I added, even if Ken was only focusing on a fundamentally correct swing, a 9-1 ratio clinic for two hours a week isn't going to maximize potential at the quickest rate.

Once I got Dr. Lee's attention, we ran through Ken's evaluation package. It turns out that even though Dr. Lee is very educated and successful; his raising athletic royalty skills were below par (no pun intended).

Dr. Lee thought that by placing his son, Ken, into the golf director's group clinic at their country club, that Ken would get the proper training for a collegiate golf career. However, the clinic was not providing Ken with the essential components needed to attain elite athletic stature. Such components would include: organizing a personalized developmental plan, assisting with stroke mechanics, arranging practice rounds, strength training sessions, scheduling tournaments, helping with equipment preparation etc. Ironically, the golf director didn't even know Ken's name.

Towards the end of our session Ken said, "Dad, it makes sense now, if putting is the worst part of my game, hitting drives and irons off the mats for two hours a week isn't even addressing my biggest flaw! We have been wasting so much time."

We customized a developmental plan and shed light on the essential components that needed to be developed in Ken's game. A goal without a plan is just a dream.

FYI: Parents, if your child is only attending a few private lessons or group clinics each week, please don't assume that a world class developmental plan is in the works. Also, please don't expect high level results.

"Sitting down and setting a goal is like fueling up the car before a long road trip. It's only the beginning."

"Achieving goals requires flexibility and compromise."

"GOALS SHOULD BE BEYOND YOUR CURRENT REACH YET REALISTIC AND UNDER A TIMELINE."

"Goals should be put in writing to serve as an organizational blue print and as a daily reminder of the group's mission."

"DO SOMETHING EVERYDAY THAT PUSHES YOU CLOSER TO YOUR GOALS."

"SADLY, MANY GREAT PHYSICAL ATHLETES BELIEVE THEY DON'T NEED A DEVELOPMENTAL PLAN BECAUSE THEY'RE MORE GIFTED THAN THEIR NEIGHBORS DOWN THE STREET."

"Don't let short term junior goals cloud your player's long term development."

"PARENTS, REMEMBER THAT GOALS AND DREAMS COME WITH MISTAKES, SETBACKS, HARDSHIPS AND TEARS. IT IS PART OF THE RIDE."

"To attain long term goals, one must lose a few battles in order to win the war."

GUTS

"Great athletes trust the visible facts as well as their intuition."

"One's nurturing, education and life experiences bond together to provide that gut feeling."

"Your gut feeling isn't always correct. It could be the demons on your shoulder doing their best to derail you."

"OUR THOUGHTS AND FEELINGS ENTER OUR BRAINS LIKE AIRPLANES COMING AND GOING THROUGH A BUSY AIRPORT. YOU HAVE THE ABILITY TO CHOOSE WHAT TRIP TO TAKE."

H

HABITS

"CONSISTENT PRE-GAME ROUTINES & RITUALS ARE HABITS WORTH DEVELOPING."

"Delete comfortable, lazy habits or they will surely derail your best effort."

"TAKE GREAT CARE OF YOUR GOOD HABITS AND IN CRUNCH TIME, THEY WILL TAKE GREAT CARE OF YOU."

"Habits aren't simply physical; they are mental and emotional as well."

"PROPER PREPARATION IS A ROUTINE- A HABIT. IT'S ALSO THE SECRET ANTIDOTE TO PERFORMANCE ANXIETY."

"Practicing the art of focusing intently 'in the moment' for a few hours is a mental, emotional habit worth developing."

"THE QUALITY OF PRACTICE DAY HABITS DETERMINES GAME DAY HABITS."

"Good habits performed religiously become second nature and that's when playing in the zone occurs."

"MAKE IT A HABIT TO APPLY IMAGERY EACH NIGHT BEFORE GOING TO SLEEP. WITH THE LIGHTS OFF AND EVERYTHING QUIET, VISUALIZE YOURSELF PERFORMING FREELY AT YOUR PEAK LEVEL."

HONESTY & HONOR

"SHOW HONOR AND RESPECT FOR THE LESSONS LEARNED FROM THE SPORT. THEY WILL SERVE YOU FOR A LIFE TIME."

"Some parents get so caught up in the glory of one upping their neighbors, family and friends that they embellish the time and effort their child is truly putting into their development."

"Parents that purposely deceive their child's coach and trainer about their child's actual training efforts are damaging their child's self-confidence and stunting their growth."

"Be wary of the coach and/or sports academy that purposefully keeps athletes away from competition as long as possible…Without measurable developmental results, there is no accountability."

"Being honest with oneself is the key to confidence."

"All the lies you told about training properly will spill out during competition."

"PARENTS, YOUR WORDS HAVE TO MATCH YOUR ACTIONS IF YOU WANT YOUR CHILD TO DO THE SAME."

"Be honest about your work ethic, perseverance, attitude and commitment."

"CLASSY ATHLETES THANK THE COACHES, THE REFEREES AND THE FACILITY STAFF AFTER EACH EVENT."

|

IMPROVEMENT

LESSON: **Dummy Up**

Alexandra has a great memory for a 13-year-old. You can tell her ten soccer facts while she's playing a video game and she'll recall all ten of the topics days later. She's off the charts book smart too. She's maintained her straight A GPA throughout her education. Alexandra attends the most advanced prestigious prep school in Chicago and she loves soccer.

Alexandra's passionate dedication to soccer is not proving successful. Her mom says, "The other kids are running like the wind to the ball and our Alex is slow as molasses. Although she is a very fast runner, when she is playing, she seems to be frozen and unable to run."

During their visit to Southern California to complete our Customized Evaluation Package, we talked about true intelligence in sports and how it relates to different personality profiles.

Alexandra is a soft ISTJ. By soft I mean less rigid in some of the categories. Alexandra is a good physical athlete. Her issues lie in what neuroscientists call cognitive processing speed. Simply put, there are far too many thoughts swimming in her head and she processes all of them before choosing the correct pathway.

On the field, sports intelligence is the ability to assess only the problem and stepping into only the solution within milliseconds. Alexandra's issue is that she's been nurtured by her extremely detail oriented SJ (brain type) mother. Alexandra has constantly and consistently witnessed thirteen years of overthinking, over stressing and worrying over every possible problem. This nurturing has developed hesitation in her decision making ability. The hesitation stems from the fear of possibly being wrong. ISTJ's personalities despise being wrong.

Alexandra's inborn judger personality profile along with her mother's extremely rigid judger personality profile have combined to make Alexandra to appear mentally and physically slow on the soccer field. This is a great example of a parental blunder and the child getting all the blame.

Alexandra's delayed reactions stem from her mother's obsession with worrying about dozens of possible future problems. Of course, most of which never happen. To put it bluntly, her mom's hang ups have become the reason for her hesitation. Interestingly, when I asked Alexandra to simply run from point A to point B and back she performs brilliantly. This is what I call a blocked learning drill. Alexandra's mind is preset with the pathway so there is no brain speed required, no optional thoughts to cause hesitation, no possibility of running the wrong way and appearing stupid.

Alexandra's solution began with explaining to her, her genetic predisposition and her parental nurturing issues and then we began the slow process of developing her flexible skills sports intelligence. I asked Alexandra's parents to help with a daily drill to improve Alexandra's reaction speed. The parents were to number four spots in the backyard. Alex was to stand at a home base position and run to the randomly called spot and then returned to her starting point between each call. This drill trains her brain to only focus on her quick decision making ability and to trust her anticipation and intuition.

By clearing out all of the thoughts that were pulling Alex away from executing what the second demands, she was able to "dummy up" and get into the self-trusting flow that comes from not over thinking. Alex went on to become an all-star soccer player and is in the starting line up as a freshman on her varsity high school team.

Special Note: Children aren't born with performance anxiety. Parental stressors are most often the cause of athletes' anxiety/panic issues even before their game begins. It is important to remind parents that their behaviors and words are often the actual cause of the child's fear.

"TRUST THAT OPPONENTS FROM AROUND THE WORLD ARE WORKING HARDER AND SMARTER TO IMPROVE."

"Due to the evolution of sports and athletes, being content and satisfied means you're falling behind...while you are resting, others are improving."

"Please choose customized deliberate practice versus going through the typical training regimes."

"Be prepared to raise your practice level as you enter into higher levels of competition."

"VIEW JUNIOR COMPETITION AS AN INFORMATION GATHERING MISSION AND NOT AS A LIFE OR DEATH EVENT."

"CONSISTENT WINS COME FROM CONSISTENT IMPROVEMENT."

"Year-round dedication, focus and improvement are mandatory if collegiate level sports are desired. Seasonal athletic activity is reserved for the hobbyist."

"Insist on improving all of the components vital to world class athletic stature. Spending 100% of your child's developmental time on fundamentals is a mistake."

"Parents, you can't put your child in with the pack (group training) AND expect them to outperform the pack."

INNER CHATTER (SELF TALK)

"Prior to match play, winners focus on their strengths and losers focus on their excuses for possible failures."

"POSITIVE SELF-TALK HELPS DEVELOP SELF-TRUST AND BUILDS CONFIDENCE."

"SELF-TRUST IS MANDATORY WHEN THE GAME IS ON THE LINE. EDUCATE SELF-TRUST."

"Nurture positive affirmations from an early age."

"Pregame positive self-talk is found in visualization/imagery."

INTEGRITY

LESSON: **Type A Personality Parents**

The phrase "Type A Personality" is a relic of psychology dating back to the 1950's. The reason why it relates here is because it is the most common parental personality of high performance athletes. This can be both beneficial and harmful to developing athletes.

The positive side of possessing this personality is that the parent tends to be highly competitive, achievement oriented, ambitious, focused, diligent, organized and willing to go the distance in order to achieve success for their children. On the negative side, Type A personalities can be a bit too aggressive, obsessive, willing to bend the rules if it benefits their cause, demanding, rigid, impatient, anxious and often insensitive to their child's needs.

If a diligent parental manager crosses the line and becomes an overbearing negative influence on the development of the child, it's in the child's best interest to seek help. The modern term for these slightly over-the-top moms and dads is

"Helicopter Parent." You know you're a helicopter parent if you have your child's coach's cell phone numbers on your speed dial. When your child loses in an event, your first thought is "Which coach is to blame?"...When your child doesn't feel like preparing properly for an event and you jump in and do it for them...When your child meets a conflict and should be "thinking for themselves" to find the resolution, but you solve it for them.

If these ring true, you just may be stunting the actual growth you seek. If so, at the first sign of stress, don't run to the immediate rescue. Give your children time to solve their own problems. Scale back to "assisting" your child with their life's quest versus doing everything for them. Lastly, nurture and praise their problem solving skills. After all, sports can only teach valuable life lessons if you allow them to learn in the process.

"PARENTS, REMEMBER THAT CHILDREN DO WHAT YOU DO, NOT WHAT YOU SAY. IF RULES DON'T APPLY TO YOU, THEN DON'T EXPECT RULES TO APPLY TO THEM."

"Parents, if you are stressed out simply driving to the event, can you imagine the stress you are adding to your child? What signals are you sending?"

"HIGH PERFORMANCE SPORTS DEMANDS INTEGRITY."

"Once your actions become questionable and your words become lies, you can kiss athletic royalty goodbye."

INTELLIGENCE

"TRUE INTELLIGENCE IN SPORTS ISN'T ABOUT MEMORIZING WHAT YOU READ IN BOOKS. IT'S ASSESSING THE PROBLEM AND FINDING THE SOLUTION AT THE QUICKEST RATE."

"Sports Intelligence is only thinking about what the moment demands. Overthinking in sports is a sign of poor sports intelligence."

"PEAK PERFORMERS DON'T AGONIZE OVER PAST MISTAKES."

"A SIGN OF A HIGH SPORTS IQ IS DETERMINED BY HOW QUICKLY YOU RECOGNIZE AND THEN SHUT DOWN THE OPPONENT'S WINNING PLAYS."

"Find what works, even if you have to borrow it from the others."

"INTELLIGENT PERFORMANCES BEGIN WITH STARTING PRE-GAME PREPARATION ON A HAPPY, POSITIVE NOTE."

"Develop a high IQ for your sport. Be a student of the game. Constantly search YouTube and educational web sites for applicable fresh new ideas to stay ahead of the crowd."

"LIST YOUR STRENGTHS AND WEAKNESSES. THEN ORGANIZE PLAYS AND PATTERNS TO EXPOSE YOUR STRENGTHS WHILE HIDING YOUR WEAKNESSES."

"List the strengths and weaknesses of your opponents. Then organize ways to expose their weaknesses as well as ways to avoid their strengths."

INTIMIDATION

"Positive posture and poise under stress sends a powerful message."

"If you keep your composure and appear unflappable, the opponent will most likely crack."

"OPPONENTS WHO DEEPLY BELIEVE THEY DON'T HAVE THE PHYSICAL TALENT TO BEAT YOU WILL OFTEN EMPLOY GAMESMANSHIP TO INTIMIDATE."

"WHEN JUNIORS ARE INTIMIDATED BY THE MOMENT THEY OFTEN MANIFEST A SICKNESS, A FEELING OF BEING OVER TIRED OR AN INJURY."

K

KNOWLEDGE/POWER

"Adapting to changes is game day intelligence."

"KNOWLEDGE GAINED THROUGH SPORTS MAKES YOU A BETTER PLAYER IN THE GAME OF LIFE."

"If knowledge is being book smart and intelligence is being street smart, then athletic royalty demands intelligence."

"Knowledge really isn't that powerful without action."

"If knowledge is developed through disciplined learning, where does learning come from? Learning comes from experience. Athletes generally learn more from losses than wins."

"ATTITUDE, KNOWLEDGE AND EFFORT EQUAL SUCCESS."

"An athlete's 'hardware package' is the strength of their body. An athlete's 'software package' is the strength of their mind. Most parents and coaches only focus on the development of their child's hardware."

"Knowledge without the guts to compete is wasted."

L

LISTEN

"The ability to listen and digest meaningful data is a learned behavior."

"LISTEN WITH YOUR 'EYES' TO PICK UP FACIAL EXPRESSIONS AND BODY LANGUAGE."

"The ability to read between the lines while listening is key. Often passive aggressive people speak in code."

"PAY ATTENTION TO THE ANNUNCIATION, THE TONE OF VOICE AND THE ATTITUDE THAT IS BEING DELIVERED ALONG WITH THE WORDS."

"IN MOST CONVERSATIONS, THE MOST COMMON WAY OF NOT HEARING SOMETHING IMPORTANT IS BY THINKING ABOUT YOUR OWN CLEVER RESPONSE INSTEAD OF LISTENING."

"Teens don't listen because they're still young enough to think they know it all."

LOSERS

LESSON: **The Blessings of Unanswered Prayers**

David is a San Diego real estate agent. He makes most workaholics seem lazy. Getting a call from him mid-afternoon was unusual. David tried to calm his nerves by taking a few deep breaths and then frantically explained the new "life and death" drama facing his family.

"Frank, Jessie's just told me she's quitting! After everything we put into this! How could she want to be such a loser? She is so talented." David went on and on about the time, money, blood, sweat and tears that went into his daughter's diving career. "We've been planning, hoping and praying that she'd be an NCAA Division 1 college diver. She's been diving since she was 8 years old!"

Jessie told us she's not happy spending so much of her time training. She says she's miserable because she doesn't want to let us down, but she also doesn't want to chase our dream any longer."

I had never experienced a father so distraught over his daughter's decision to quit her junior diving team.

Fast forward three years…Jessie has news for her folks. "Mom, Dad, I just got my combined test results on my SAT: I got an 800 on all 3 sections- mathematics, critical reading, and writing. I GOT A 2400! Now I've got a real shot at Harvard or Stanford."

Jessie is crazy excited. She goes on to tell them, "You know my Advanced Chemistry Experimentation and Instrumentation Class? Well, I've been mixing cancer medicine with a polymer that attaches to nanoparticles. See, they fasten themselves to cancer cells that actually show up on MRI's allowing Doctors to actually see tumors! The infrared light then melts the polymer, releases the medicine; killing the cancer! It's super cool because it leaves the healthy cells unharmed…"

Life is funny when it comes to the larger callings and bigger pictures. Yes, Jessie isn't going to be an All-American swimmer, but the life lessons learned through sports served her well. She's a bit busy right now… curing cancer.

"Ambition, self-discipline, taking responsibility and a solid work ethic are the core ingredients found in winners"

"A LOSS DOESN'T MAKE YOU A LOSER…IF YOU'RE WILLING TO LEARN FROM IT."

"EMOTIONALLY WEAK COMPETITORS FAKE INJURIES TO AVOID THE BLAME OF A POSSIBLE UPCOMING LOSS."

"Parents unintentionally allow their children to train improperly and then blame their children for having no confidence."

"NATURAL BORN ATHLETES OFTEN LOSE DUE TO THEIR LACK OF WORK ETHIC."

"The definition of a loser in sports is not someone that loses in competition, but someone who chooses not to prepare properly."

LUCK

"Luck plays a major role in sports. Good luck only happens when solid preparation meets opportunity."

"Often doing the right things provides the opportunity for good luck."

"FOR GOOD LUCK TO FIND YOU- YOU HAVE TO BE PRESENT. NOBODY EVER WON AN EVENT BY CHOOSING TO STAY AT HOME. "

"Overcoming bad luck is what puts you in position to receive good luck."

"GOOD LUCK IS DILIGENCE IN DISGUISE."

"Maybe your so called temporary bad luck actually saved you from disaster."

"Being born with the personality to make it happen is good luck."

"FINDING SOMEONE TO PUSH YOU OUTSIDE OF YOUR ROUTINES AND HABITS IS LUCKY BECAUSE THAT'S WHERE GROWTH LIVES."

M

MENTAL TOUGHNESS

"THE X'S AND O'S OF STRATEGY AND TACTICS IS THE MENTAL GAME."

"Blocking out internal and external irreverent stimuli is mental toughness."

"Be aware of your thoughts during competition. Are they in the past, present or future? Are they relevant to the mission at hand? If not, delete them immediately."

"MENTAL TOUGHNESS IS BEING HONEST WITH YOUR ASSESSMENT IN YOUR PERFORMANCE CRITIQUE."

"Being self-reliant and responsible for your performance is mental toughness."

"Perseverance and resiliency is mental toughness."

"MENTAL TOUGHNESS IS THE ANALYTICAL DECISIONS MADE UNDER STRESS."

"Mental toughness is focus control. It is saying 'Not Now' to inappropriate thoughts."

"MENTAL TOUGHNESS IS NOT OVERTHINKING. OVER THINKERS CREATE STRESS, NERVOUSNESS, WORRY AND FEAR."

MISTAKE MANAGEMENT

LESSON: **Why Asking Your Kid to Give 110% Is Wrong**

Gloria and her daughter Jenny were in the process of hiring a new full time private coach. Like cartons of milk, often coaches have expiration dates. They all have a bag of developmental tricks and once you've heard them over and over again and your growth has stalled, it may be time to move on.

During our phone consultation, Gloria mentioned their current coach was stuck on the singular, component of perfect fundamentals. His motto was "Get your fundamentals down 110% and that alone will be enough to take home the gold." Gloria said, "The problem is that Jenny can perform brilliantly in practice, but comes unglued in real events."

I completely understood and let Gloria know that Jenny is suffering from a very common and curable poor developmental plan. Although Jenny could be 110% fundamentally perfect in practice, real competition introduces additional physical, mental and emotional forces resulting in performance anxieties.

Gloria agreed that Jenny gets extremely nervous and fearful before competition. As we talked, she shared that Jenny's over arousal leads to over thinking, tight muscle contractions, less fluid movements, hesitations and silly routine mistakes that do not exist in practice. I asked Gloria to begin talking to Jenny about changing her attempts to be 110% perfect with simply trying to be only 90% excellent. This will allow Jenny to accept tiny performance flaws and quickly move on. Knowing that you don't need to be perfect every day and can still be a champion is very de-stressing.

Focusing on excellent performances allows you to leave perfection behind. Asking a child to be 110% (better than perfect every time) seems rather silly and unattainable doesn't it? In essence, her old coach had great intentions but was actually psychologically setting Jenny up for consistent failure. With that in mind, Gloria began to look for a mental and emotional expert coach to assist Jenny with the next stage in her career.

Remember parents, performers and athletes should seek consistent excellent performances not consistent perfect performances.

"Game day performance logs are an excellent way to identify strengths and weaknesses."

"GAME DAY VIDEO ANALYSIS PROVIDES ASSESSMENT OF YOUR PLAYER'S TECHNICAL EFFICIENCIES, MENTAL AND EMOTIONAL CONTROL UNDER STRESS, MOVEMENT, FITNESS, AGILITY, FOCUS, STRENGTHS AND WEAKNESSES AS WELL AS OPPONENT PROFILING."

"Managing mistakes requires forgiveness and the ability to have great short term memory loss."

"REOCCURRING NIGHTMARES ARE MISTAKES THAT TEND TO BE REPEATED GAME AFTER GAME."

"IT'S NOT THE SINGLE MISTAKE THAT HURTS AS MUCH AS HOW THE ATHLETE RECOVERS FROM THE ERROR."

"Most mistakes come from two opposing energies, overcooking and undercooking."

MOMENTS (TIPPING POINTS)

"TIPPING POINTS ARE THOSE SPECIAL MOMENTS OF STRUGGLE WHEN BOTH SIDES GRAB HOLD OF THE ENERGY AND PLAY TUG-OF-WAR."

"EACH ATHLETIC EVENT PROVIDES A FEW CHANCES TO RISE ABOVE THE CROWD AND DO SOMETHING INCREDIBLE. THESE ARE THE TIPPING POINTS WHEN THE GAME HANGS IN THE BALANCE. PREPARE

PHYSICALLY, MENTALLY AND EMOTIONALLY FOR THOSE MOMENTS, FOR THEY WILL DEFINE YOU."

"At the top of every level in every sport, there are a few defining moments when taking offensive action is required in order to allow you to pass into the higher level."

"BEGIN GAME DAY WITH THE FEELING THAT THERE'S NO OTHER PLACE I'D RATHER BE THAN HERE TODAY."

"COMPETITION DAY IS JOYOUS IF YOU HAVE PREPARED PROPERLY, TERRIFYING IF YOU HAVEN'T..."

"APPROACH THE TIPPING POINTS IN COMPETITION WITH STRENGTH IN ATTITUDE, CONVICTION, POSITIVE BODY LANGUAGE AND MOST OF ALL WITH AN AURA OF CONFIDENCE. WINNING BEGINS WITH AN INTIMIDATING PRESENCE."

MOTIVATION

"MOTIVATION IS THE FORCE THAT INSTIGATES THE WORK."

"GREAT MOTIVATORS LOOK FOR THE INTRINSIC FORCES. THESE ARE THE SECRET BUTTONS. WHEN PUSHED PROPERLY, ATHLETES FLY."

"Each of the 16 personality profiles or brain types may require very different motivation and training."

"Motivation for some is the joy of winning. For others it's the pain of losing."

"PARENTS, INSTILL LOVE AND RESPECT FIRST BECAUSE CONTINUOUS MOTIVATION REQUIRES A POSITIVE RELATIONSHIP."

N

NEGATIVITY

LESSON: Negatron Baton

Mr. Gracy runs his family's extremely successful Auto Mall in Miami Florida. You name it, they sell it, from those tiny Cracker Jack Coopers which they sell to yuppies to Rolls Royce and Bentley's custom made for the snow birds. He says that he makes a killing each year on the New Yorker's trying to one-up one another.

Sadly, that's not the only thing Jack Gracy is killing.

Jack possesses a common parental Type A personality that believes his child should be athletic royalty…yesterday. The problem with Jack is that he can't see the good in his very own incredible good fortune and would rather see the negative in most situations. His toxic pessimism is what he brings front and center to his son's swimming career.

If you meet Jack's middle son, Jackson Gracy, you'd quickly say that he has the same dreaded disease. Thirteen-year-old Jackson can put a negative spin on just about everything. To Jackson, negativity is second nature because he has been nurtured with this personality trait since he was old enough to talk.

The Gracy family flew me to South Beach for a typical weekend evaluation session. By the end of day one, I quickly realized that the first order of business was to get the entire family involved. If young Jackson was ever to be coachable in any endeavor he'd have to buy into and succeed in a life changing epiphany that optimism is a choice. For that, I needed the entire family's assistance.

I asked Mr. Gracy to gather his wife Marcy and their four kids: Kelly, Shaun, Jackson and Daniel for a 7 p.m. meeting. Reluctantly with his skepticism in full check, Jack ordered his family into their massive family room in their estate along the intercoastal waterway. At 7 p.m. sharp, they all sat down. I couldn't help to ask jokingly to take a picture of this glorious sight. All six of them were present, but staring intently at their own cell phones without a single bit of interest in the proceedings.

I began by thanking them for turning off their phones and supporting my efforts to assess Jackson's developmental plan to swim in college and later make the U.S. Olympics team. Right then, Jackson's younger siblings Kelly and Shaun burst into sarcastic laughter at the thought of Jackson's swimming goals. That was my cue.

I began by asking if anyone noticed the dark cloud of negative, pessimistic, cynical, attitudes, behaviors and overtones that are present in the family. The silence was finally broken by Marcy in a quiet monotone "Yes." Once the silence was broken, it was safe to speak the truth.

My strategy was life changing yet simple. Anyone and everyone in the room were free to say "Spin it" to anyone else if they felt that the other family member was being negative in any way. Quickly the room changed from scared silence to smiles.

I began with a negative comment, "It's too hot and humid down here in Florida"... That was followed by a room full of halfhearted "Spin it's". We spent the next half hour passing the negatron baton around the room followed by laughter and "Spin it's". Mrs. Gracy was up next, "I'm too tired to cook"... "SPIN IT!" Kelly jumped in "My knees are sore, so I can't train tomorrow"... "SPIN IT!" Shaun said, "I don't feel like doing my homework"... "SPIN IT!" Even Jack chimed in,

"I'm too tired to go to work this month"…Followed by a huge "SPIN IT!!!" and laughter.

At weekend's end, I asked the family to run an experiment for an entire week. For every negative comment voiced, everyone was allowed to say "Spin-it" and then identify a positive aspect to the situation. I followed up by asking Jack to call me the following weekend to report their findings.

One week later Jack said that he, Marcy and the kids were astonished by the sheer number of pessimistic, negative behaviors and comments they witnessed each day. "It must have been hundreds of negatives the first few days", he said. "Interestingly as the negatives were exposed and we became aware of them, the family began to consciously make positive changes."

Jack said, "This 'Spin-it' game worked so well that I've added it to our Auto business plan. Spinning the pessimism upside down into optimism seems to be contagious. For some individuals, pessimism is so deeply ingrained that they are unaware how negatively they view the world."

Fast forward four years and Jackson was the team captain on his college swim team!

"Pessimism, cynicism and negativity are poison."

"NEGATIVE PEOPLE EVENTUALLY SUCK YOU INTO THEIR WORLD."

"Negatrons are toxic people who are eager to spread their darkness."

"NEGATIVE PEOPLE DESTROY EVERYBODY'S CONFIDENCE AND SELF-ESTEEM."

"Some athletes create their own drama, and then complain about it."

"Sadly, negative people believe they are in reality and positive people are out of touch."

"IT ONLY TAKES ONE NEGATIVE COMMENT FROM A PARENT TO UNRAVEL EVERYTHING A COACH HAS BEEN BUILDING."

NUTRITION AND HYDRATION

LESSON: **Running on Empty**

It is 7:00 am at the Riviera Tennis Club in Palm Springs, California. The top tennis players from around the country arrived last night for the first round of the prestigious National Championships.

Walking through a hall of the west wing of the hotel and I can hear Leslie through their door, "Mom…STOP!!! I'm not hungry. Stop forcing me to eat! I'm too nervous. I don't feel hungry!" This has been an on-going pre-match battle for Leslie and her mom Carol and this time would prove catastrophic.

Trying her best to avoid an emotional battle right before Leslie's match, Carol gives up on her job of making sure Leslie is prepared for a three hour battle in the blazing Palm Springs heat. "So much for your nutrition and hydration requirements... I give up", cries Carol.

The first match on Court 7 went to three tough sets so Leslie begins her scheduled 9:00 am match around 10:00 am. Leslie, being a top seed and a far superior athlete jumps out to a commanding 6-2 first set lead. Midway through the second set her wheels to fall off. Leslie can't seem to focus; her body feels uncoordinated and shaky. She complains of feeling dizzy, like she's going to faint. Leslie begins to make unforced errors left and right. She drops the second set 4-6. At the start of the critical third set the time is now 11:30 am. Leslie hasn't fueled her body since last night's dinner at 6:30 pm, which was 16 hours ago.

Guess who goes down in flames losing the third set 1-6? You got it-Leslie! Her disappointing first round loss was directly related to her stubbornness to fuel her body properly.

"The ultimate athletic goal with respect to nutrition is to maintain a healthy balanced diet day in and day out with special attention to proper nutrition prior, during and after competition."

"HYDRATION IS MANDATORY FOR OPTIMAL PERFORMANCE. DEHYDRATION OF 1% OF YOUR BODY WEIGHT COMPROMISES PHYSIOLOGIC FUNCTIONS. DEHYDRATION OF 3% INCREASES THE ATHLETE'S RISK OF DEVELOPING CRAMPS OR HEAT EXHAUSTION. DEHYDRATION OF 5 % OR MORE OF

THE ATHLETE'S BODY WEIGHT CAN BE LIFE
THREATENING."

*"Drinking several full strength sugar sports drinks per
day can add hundreds of unnecessary calories to an
athlete's daily dietary intake."*

*"It is important that you don't begin competition with
an empty or totally full stomach. A small snack or mini
meal is optimal for peak performance."*

"IDEAL PERFORMANCE REQUIRES PROPER NUTRITION
AND HYDRATION. IT IS NOT JUST WHAT YOU EAT; IT
IS WHEN YOU EAT IT."

*"Consuming high-quality lean proteins directly after
training and/or competition enables the body to recover
and repair damaged muscle tissue more efficiently."*

*"A small meal of complex carbohydrates, low to
moderate in protein, low in fat and low in fiber shortly
before competition or training will improve
performance. High protein, fats and fiber take longer to
digest and may cause intestinal distress during play."*

"ZERO CARBOHYDRATE DIETS DO NOT SUPPORT HIGH PERFORMANCE ATHLETES. HEALTHY CARBOHYDRATES ARE ESSENTIAL FOR AN ATHLETE'S PHYSICAL AND MENTAL PERFORMANCE."

"It is never a good idea to try new foods, drinks or supplements just before competition."

O

OPPORTUNITY

"BEING GIVEN GREAT OPPORTUNITIES BEFORE THE HARD WORK IS PUT IN IS LIKE RECEIVING A GIFT YOU CANNOT OPEN."

"CHAMPIONS TRAIN LIKE CHAMPIONS WAY BEFORE THEY EVER BECOME CHAMPIONS."

"Positive people with a 'can do' attitude seem to seek out and find more opportunities."

"Opportunities find you after your famous, not before."

"THE WINNING ORDER FOR SUCCESS IS PREPARATION, OPPORTUNITY AND EXECUTION."

OPTIMISM

"IF OPTIMISM IS THE SHIP'S MOTOR; PESSIMISM IS THE SHIP'S ANCHOR."

"Determined optimistic people suffer setbacks and heartbreak. They simply choose to be resilient."

"OPTIMISM IS DELIVERED BY THE WORDS YOU CHOOSE, TONE OF VOICE, FACIAL EXPRESSION AND BODY LANGUAGE."

"IMPACT YOUR CHILD'S MORAL CODE, ATTITUDE AND PRODUCTIVITY BY SELLING OPTIMISM."

"Parents remember: children pick up every signal you're sending."

"BEING OPTIMISTIC IS A PROGRAMMABLE CHOICE."

"Some people have a genetic predisposition to always seek the negative. Others have been nurtured with this 'dreaded disease'. What traits are you developing in your children?"

ORGANIZATION

LESSON: Israel Tennis Centers

While consulting in Israel, I had the opportunity to train sports psychologist, tennis coaches, players and parents at several beautiful Israel Tennis Centers.

I had the privilege of meeting one extremely insightful individual heading the programs in Kiryat Shemona, Israel, named Shaul Zohar. Shaul is an excellent coach and mentor. His teachings go beyond tennis and nurture life skills like organization, time management, scheduling, perseverance, work ethic, punctuality and optimism, to list a few.

I sat down with his 10-13 year old high performance group. I threw out typical questions and surprisingly they had all the answers and then some. I asked about their weekly components:

"How many hours a week do you spend on off-court tennis specific training?" "2.5 hours in the gym and 3 hours doing speed and agility work," replied Moses.

"How many hours do you spend developing your primary and secondary strokes?" "4 hours on the primary, 3 hours on our secondary," said Paul.

Match play versus pushers? Pattern repetition? Designing and rehearsing between point rituals? Handling gamesmanship? …Whatever I threw at Shaul's group, accurate and precise answers flowed from the mouths of these young players.

Typically, when I ask these very same questions to parents, players and coaches at my workshops, seminars and summits the answer is… "Aaahh …What's that?"

Customizing your child's developmental plan and systematically organizing it is the parent's initial job.

Dropping them off at a clinic or team practice isn't going to produce Athletic Royalty. Parents, you should plan on making the time to manage your child's career unless you are paying a top coach like Shaul to manage it for you.

"A CUSTOMIZED ORGANIZATIONAL BLUE-PRINT IS YOUR CHILD'S NAVIGATIONAL SYSTEM. IT MAXIMIZES POTENTIAL AT THE QUICKEST RATE."

"Take responsibility for your schedules, work ethic, efforts, words & actions."

"EXCUSES, ALIBIS AND BLAMING ARE THE HIDDEN ENEMY IN ANY SPORT."

"Organizational blue-prints are jumping off points. They're not written in stone. Stay flexible and adapt as needed."

"A well-organized athlete can train 20 hours a week and still have plenty of time for a social life."

"IF YOUR CHILD'S DEVELOPMENTAL PLAN IS PERFECTLY ORGANIZED, RUNNING 100% SMOOTH AND EVERYTHING IS CALMLY UNDER CONTROL, CHANCES ARE; YOU'RE NOT PROGRESSING FAST ENOUGH."

"Organizing A, B and even C game plans is part of high performance preparation."

"LIST PROBABLE DERAILMENTS AND THEN PRE-SET PROTOCOLS FOR THEIR SOLUTIONS."

"Pay attention to the nuances and styles of your opponents and customize your preparation."

"Periodization training is knowing not just what to fix, but when to fix it."

OVERCONFIDENCE

"IN SPORTS, THERE'S A WORLD OF DIFFERENCE BETWEEN CONTROLLED AGGRESSION AND RECKLESS AGGRESSION. OFTEN RECKLESS AGGRESSION STEMS FROM OVERCONFIDENCE. "

"Undeserved overconfidence leads to spotty training which leads to losses."

"OVERCONFIDENCE OFTEN COMES IN THE FORM OF UNDERESTIMATING THE OPPOSITION."

"Often looking past early round lesser opponents in a draw leads to early round losses."

"Overconfident athletes feel they can beat the odds with reckless, low percentage plays on a daily basis."

"TO STOMP OUT OVERCONFIDENCE SIMPLY TAKE THE BIG FISH FROM THEIR SMALL POND TO SWIM IN A BIGGER POND."

P

PASSION

"Parents, nurture passion for the sport, it leads to commitment."

"IF HARD WORK IS THE ENGINE THAT PROPELS AN ATHLETE FORWARD, PASSION IS THE FUEL."

"PASSION, LIKE OPTIMISM, IS CONTAGIOUS."

"Be passionate about learning and growing, which will push you past your personal boundaries."

"SOME ATHLETES HAVE AN INNATE PASSION FOR THE SPORT. OTHERS HAVE TO NURTURE AND GROW PASSION."

"Young athletes shouldn't be concerned about the realities of 'going pro'- let them dream big."

PATIENCE

"The 10,000 hour rule is a terrific guideline that requires patience and perseverance."

"Enjoy the experience of competition versus hectically rushing through it."

"IT TAKES PERSISTENCE AND PATIENCE TO RAISE ATHLETIC ROYALTY."

"PARENTS, IF YOU HAVE A GREAT COACH, PATIENCE IS THE ABILITY TO LET THE COACH DO THE COACHING. IF YOU HAVE A LOUSY COACH...WELL?"

"PATIENCE IS GOOD NATURED TOLERANCE."

"Sometimes in order to nurture independence, accountability and problem solving skills, parents have to simply allow their children to occasionally blow it."

"Choose patience instead of anger and you'll avoid regret."

"PATIENCE IS IGNORING YOUR INNER CRAZY."

PARENTAL OVER COACHING

LESSON: **The Cause of Performance Anxiety**

Pressure from years of unhealthy parental nurturing often takes its toll. Performance anxieties stem from athletes who subconsciously focus on the years of pessimistic nurturing as they recount the negative possibilities of failure versus the optimistic possibilities of playing at their peak performance level.

Why do some athletes choke, panic, play in fear, or play so nervous that they can't perform? Why does pressure seem to affect some juniors and not others? The answer lies not only in the player's pre game routines and rituals but in the parents as well.

Often parents unknowingly add incredible amounts of stress that causes performance anxiety with their chosen words. If this story hits close to home, read the eBook Match Day Preparation. It covers the do's and don'ts in regards to the state of mind of the athlete and the athlete's parents on game day. (www.maximizingtennispotential.com)

Game time parental blunders include these types of horrible pep talks:

"If you win today, it'll be the biggest win of your career...You have to win!"

"We spent $2,500.00 to get you here this weekend... Don't blow it"

"If you lose to her, you'll surely lose your spot on the varsity team and any chance of your UCLA scholarship."

"Remember, your ranking will drop if you don't win this tournament and you won't qualify for the junior Olympic team."

"Ok, listen. You have to throw all strikes today. Don't get wild out there! These batters will rip any pitch under 80 mph so don't ease up. And remember…No walks. Do you understand? Only strikes!"

If you, your spouse or coaches are employing this type of motivational speech, the only thing you are motivating is performance anxiety.

"Just because you're anxious, nervous, and stressed out doesn't mean your child is... yet."

"PARENTS, IT'S NOT JUST THE NUMBER OF HOURS YOUR CHILD PUTS INTO THEIR SPORT. IT'S WHAT YOU AND YOUR COACHES PUT INTO THOSE HOURS."

"LIVING VICARIOUSLY THROUGH YOUR CHILD'S SPORTS SUCCESS FORCES THEM TO CARRY YOUR BOULDER ON THEIR SHOULDERS."

PERFECTIONISM

LESSON: The Fully Developed Human Brain

"It's not my fault mom! My brains not fully developed…Google it…" is the go-to excuse applied by most of my students. In our seminars, we touch upon the common research regarding the limitations of a teenager's brain. Parents, coaches and athletes get a kick out of the neurological findings in regards to a teen's inability to handle their emotions, planning, managing risks, and their inability to stay on task for hours through their teenage years.

Studies indicate that the human brain undergoes tremendous 'pruning of the neurons and myelination' (which translates to growth) through their late adolescence. While the scientific community banters over specifics, they agree that the human brain (both male and female) reaches full maturity in the early twenties.

The Institute for Highway Safety reports that teens are four times more likely to be involved in an auto accident and that's due to their underdeveloped brains. The National Institute of Health suggests that the section of the brain that restrains risky behavior is not fully developed until the age of twenty five. The bottom line with these interesting findings is that adolescent athletes are competing before the decision making center of their brains are fully developed.

The moral to the story is: Cut your athletes some slack. Don't expect your teenager to perform perfectly because they have a pretty darn good excuse. Instead, encourage excellence and don't demand perfection. Most full grown adults I know don't focus fully (100%) on their job while at work. They don't put themselves on the line in national competition. They also don't put their mind and bodies through such a rigorous growth process. Take a typical weekly schedule of a top junior athlete and my bet is that 95% of the parents couldn't make it through the first week.

I suggest you put this book down for a moment and go give your child a hug. You are a very lucky parent!

"NEVER ASK FOR PERFECTION, PERFECTION IS AN ILLUSION."

"Focus on the progress your child has made versus always complaining about how far they have to go."

"PERFECTIONISM IS AN EMOTIONAL DISEASE."

"If you want to demoralize your child, expect perfection."

"Poise under stress is the solution, perfectionism is the problem."

"Uncertainty and imperfection are a reality in junior athletics."

"Forget being perfect and work on being the best athlete you can be."

"Perfectionism leads to misery, stunts your growth and is demoralizing."

"PARENTS THAT DEMAND PERFECTION WILL RAISE PERFECTLY MISERABLE CHILDREN."

PERSEVERANCE

"PERSEVERANCE IS THE ABILITY TO HANDLE HARDSHIP."

"In most sports, perseverance under pressure trumps perfect form."

"PERSEVERANCE AND PERSISTENCE TRUMP RAW TALENT AND I.Q."

"Successful athletes find a way to win even when they're performing below their peak performance level."

"WISDOM TELLS US THAT WE NEED DEVASTATING DEFEATS TO BUILD UP OUR EMOTIONAL MUSCLES."

"Perseverance requires confidence and the will to fight-without it, technique is meaningless."

"PERSEVERANCE IS HAVING THE COURAGE TO TRY AGAIN TOMORROW."

PERSISTENCE

LESSON: **What College Coaches Seek**

I'm very lucky to get the opportunity to work with some of the NCAA's finest coaches. As guest speakers, these top coaches have shared their secrets. What are they looking for? Is it clean mechanics? Is it height or muscle mass? How important are your high school sports results? Is your child's National ranking the whole picture?

First of all, the word I hear college coaches use most is persistence. They seek players who want to improve. That means they are coachable. They seek players with families and primary junior coaches who teach life lessons and moral values as much as fundamentals. Persistence wins championships not raw talent. College coaches want to see determination and stubbornness in the player's pursuit of mastering their sport. Coaches demand persistence in their work ethic to attend class, graduate on time and to be positive team players.

Why? Because these are the ingredients of winners. Coaches seek winners to assist them in winning. They don't need good; they need great and great comes from persistence. A ton of parents aren't going to like to hear this but, they don't need a kid with potential. A kid with only potential hasn't trained persistently. They don't need unproven diamonds in the rough, they need diamonds. So how are diamonds made? They're made with persistent years of pressure.

If your long term goal is a NCAA All-American, Olympian or professional athlete your journey starts with persistence.

"Persistence demands saying no to all the other distractions."

"People who are simply persistent and ambitious make their own luck."

"IT IS NOT JUST ATHLETIC POTENTIAL COLLEGE COACHES SEEK. COLLEGE COACHES ARE LOOKING TO GIVE ATHLETIC SCHOLARSHIPS TO KIDS WHO ARE PERSISTENT, DETERMINED, OPTIMISTIC AND WILLING TO WORK."

"Normal discouraging moments don't affect the energy or enthusiasm of a persistent competitor."

"PERSISTENCE MAKES CHAMPIONS NOT TALENT. TALENT IS A DIME A DOZEN."

POISE

"Calmly handling hardships is poise under stress. Simulate stressful situations in practice to rehearse poise under pressure."

"OFTEN PHYSICALLY TALENTED ATHLETES WHO CAN'T CONTROL THEIR EMOTIONS ARE A COACH'S WORST NIGHTMARE."

"KEEPING CALM, COOL AND COLLECTED DURING TIPPING POINTS SEPARATES WINNERS FROM LOSERS."

"Poise is intimidating."

POSITIVE OUTLOOK

"In high level competition there are two very different mental, emotional approaches, playing to win and playing not to lose. The first one provides the opportunity for greatness. The second only works in the lower levels of sports because the opponents are often less developed and crazier than your child."

"The fastest way to become the best is by beating the best."

"IN ORDER TO ENJOY PERFORMING SUPERBLY, ONE MUST FIRST TRAIN SUPERBLY."

"It is unhealthy and exhausting to devote your energy to negative thoughts."

"ON A DAILY BASIS, LIST EVERYTHING GOOD ABOUT YOUR CHILD VERSUS FOCUSING EXCLUSIVELY ON THEIR FLAWS."

"AFTER A POOR PERFORMANCE, A CHILD NEEDS LOVE AND POSITIVE REMINDERS FROM THEIR PARENTS, NOT A LAUNDRY LIST OF THEIR FAILURES."

PRACTICE

"PRACTICE IN THE MANNER IN WHICH YOU'RE EXPECTED TO PERFORM."

"Practicing poor technique, inappropriate strategies and zero emotional control makes them permanent."

"GAMES ARE WON WEEKS BEFORE THE EVENT TAKES PLACE."

"Great practice makes progress ...nothing guarantees perfection."

"EFFORT IS THE MAGIC THAT MAKES PRACTICE MEANINGFUL."

"INTELLIGENT AND DELIBERATE TRAINING FOR 2 HOURS TRUMPS 6 HOURS OF UNACCOUNTABLE PRACTICE."

"At the intermediate levels and above, only practicing fundamentals year in and year out is like attending school and only taking math class all year. It's not going to develop a well-rounded individual."

PREPARATION

LESSON: The Hobbyist Family

It was in New Zealand, on a rainy winter weekend in early September, one hundred and fifty eager tennis parents gathered for my two-day summit. The event was organized by New Zealand's Educational Tennis Director, Craig Bell, to be a positive and enlightening experience. As a result, all attitude and biases were left at the front door, learning was encouraged and many long term friendships ensued!

The Jacks family really stood out. They had three junior players: Claudia, Mitchell and Mark. Mark and Mitchell were incredibly outgoing and possessed a wicked sense of humor. Claudia was a bit shy at first. She stood back and assessed the situation before jumping in. They were all a bit "loose" with their technique but also gifted with a keen sense of self confidence. Throughout the evaluation process of organizing their very own developmental plan, (on a scale of 1-10) the Jacks kids graded themselves with 10's at everything.

During the intermission, I asked their primary coach about the family. Interestingly, the kids were all below average competitors according to Tennis New Zealand's ranking process. I knew something important was missing from their training regimen.

This sparked my interested because the Jacks kids were confident, athletic and seemed to be soaking up every bit of the information I was dishing out. Before the lunch break was over I asked Mr. and Mrs. Jacks if we could chat after the afternoon session wraps up. Eagerly they agreed.

The last session of the day was an on court presentation regarding opponent profiling. In order to customize the seminar, I asked the group of about 70 juniors a question: "What style of opponent do you hate to play the most in tournament competition?" The overwhelming answer was PUSHERS! So we spent the last 45 minutes with the players, parents and primary coaches reviewing how to design patterns to defuse those pesky retrievers found in the game of tennis.

As the day wrapped up, the Jacks family and I went back into the classroom and sat down. Mrs. Jacks opened the conversation with a nice compliment, "Frank, we've learned more today than in the last 6 years of lessons." That's always a bittersweet comment for me to hear. Don't get me wrong, I enjoy a good ego boost like anyone else, but I was sad for their wasted time, money and energy. As our conversation shifted from their kid's potential to their families tennis developmental plan it became very clear that the parents had been treating their kids' tennis more like a passive hobby rather than a serious passionate goal of high performance tennis.

After reviewing the actual job descriptions required of the parents of champions, it was obvious why their talented kids weren't getting results on the tournament trail. Although tennis is a terrific hobby, there is a very, very big difference between having your children dabble in a sport a few hours a week and raising athletic royalty.

Parents, if you treat your child's sport like it's their 'thing' and not your 'thing' then you are treating it like a hobby. Hobbies are fine if you only want your child to get average 'hobby-like' results. If you are asking your child to get championship results, then you and your child have to take a full time approach- making their sport your priority before vacations, family gatherings, and parties, before almost everything.

So, the Jacks learned a valuable lesson that weekend. Parents who treat their child's sport like a passive hobby should only expect to have hobbyist and not elite competitors.

"PREPARE YOUR CHILDREN TO HANDLE ALL TYPES OF FATIGUE- PHYSICAL, MENTAL AND EMOTIONAL."

"ATHLETIC ROYALTY RESPECT THE PREPARATION PHASE."

"IF YOUR CHILD'S LACKING CONFIDENCE, LOOK INTO THEIR INADEQUATE PREPARATION."

"Nervousness, stress and fear are often directly related to poor preparation."

"Customize your child's preparation. There isn't a one size fits all preparation approach."

"Tardiness exposes a lack of respect towards the game, the coaches and teammates. Arrive early, leave the cell phone in the car and give 100% of your attention to your preparation."

PRESSURE

LESSON: **Mistake Management**

In an attempt to look deeper into the differences between professional athletes and high performance juniors, I met with my friend NBA star, Gal Mekel, point guard for the Dallas Mavericks.

Interestingly, the conversation (which can be found on www.maximizingtennis potential.com) focused on performance pressure. Most junior athletes agree that the immense pressure they feel stems mostly from the fear of making mistakes. So we spoke about ways to prevent mistakes and how to recover and restore oneself after a mistake has been committed. Gal shared his secret pre-game rituals and routines as well as his actual game mistake management recovery techniques.

Gal found yoga was the most beneficial technique to help transition him from his normal life and morph him into a game day, basketball warrior. Even before he leaves for the arena to begin the Maverick's detailed pre-game warm up routine, Gal performs his personal pregame ritual of yoga/meditation. This is his way of organizing his offensive and defensive strategies and plays (mental rehearsal), preventing the formation of performance anxieties (emotional toughness) and elongating his muscle groups in preparation for intense physical demands of competition (physical preparation)

Rituals and routines are mandatory, inflexible processes that aid the physical, mental and emotional components of professional athletes.

This pre-game, phase of proper preparation is an opportunity most juniors sadly choose not to fully administer. While Gal is putting up his wall to avoid negative contaminants, juniors are inviting them in. Mistakes under pressure are sure to follow if an athlete chooses to start the competition without a focused game plan, without seriously stretching, without elevating their heart rate and without blocking the normal pre-game anxieties of nervousness, fear, and doubt.

Gal and I then shifted the conversation to mistake management during competition. Gal shared his technique of "staying on script" while on the basketball court. We agreed that most often in high performance sports, errors come from leaving one's script (well-rehearsed systems) and going a bit "rogue."

Most nationally ranked juniors I work with have not yet designed their 'script' or top patterns and plays which allows them to apply their strengths and hide their weaknesses.

Gal then explained his routine used to handle pressure and manage his mistakes as a professional NBA player. From the mental side, Gal follows up his unforced errors on the basketball court by applying three very safe, clean plays inside his script. On the emotional level, he focuses on letting go of the mistake quickly and shifting his intent on keeping his energy high and his muscles loose. On the mental side, Gal focused on keeping his brain activity on the current task at hand. We laughed as Gal looked back at himself as a teenager and how he would have responded differently by panicking, losing confidence and second guessing himself after a routine on-court error.

In sports, there's a time for action and a time for reflection, a time to focus and a time to relax. Most gifted coaches focus their insights on the action. Without the rituals and routines used to manage mistakes, the athletic performance is at risk and left to chance.

I recommend putting the technical skill building process away for a few training sessions. Instead of working on fundamentals, spend some time developing two equally important components: preventing silly mistakes and the art of recovering from mistakes. Juniors unknowingly invite contaminants and are ill-equipped to handle the resulting mistakes. On the other hand, professionals apply rituals that help them to prevent and manage mistakes.

Decide the appropriate time to implement your athlete's customized solutions. Thinking clearly under pressure truly involves these hidden routines and rituals to manage mistakes.

"Disaster strikes when preconceived speculations don't match the reality of the competition. Regardless of your opponent's ranking (higher or lower), focus on your performance."

"HANDLING PRESSURE REQUIRES GETTING COMFORTABLE WITH BEING UNCOMFORTABLE."

"PRESSURE ISN'T THE ENEMY. FEELING PRESSURE MEANS YOU ARE IMPROVING. ENJOY IT!"

"Champions accept that pressure is part of competition. It is the exact drama they seek and train for...."

"Overcoming pressure forms character."

"ATHLETES WHO PREPARE PROPERLY DON'T NEED TO PANIC AND CHASE GREATNESS. IT'S ALREADY RESTING QUIETLY INSIDE THEM."

"PRESSURE, FEAR AND STRESS OFTEN COME FROM OBSESSING ABOUT POSSIBLE FAILURES WHICH, SADLY BECOMES THEIR SELF-FULFILLING PROPHECY."

PROCRASTINATION

"Athletes with a fear of the unknown or who are resistant to change often procrastinate."

"Procrastinators should start with short term goal setting like simple daily routines."

"A great way to stop procrastinating is to set time frames for each goal."

"LAZINESS FEELS GOOD NOW, BUT HURTS IN THE LONG RUN."

"PROCRASTINATION KEEPS YOU MEDIOCRE."

"Procrastination leads to crisis mode preparation which often leads to poor results."

"PROCRASTINATE NOW... PANIC IN COMPETITION."

"A junior world class athlete only has a few years of shelf life. Most juniors do not fail because they are not good enough; they fail because they run out of time due to years of procrastination."

"A GIFTED ATHLETE + PROCRASTINATION = NOTHING."

R

RESILIENCE

"DURING COMPETITION, IT'S THE SPEED THAT YOU RECOVER FROM MISTAKES THAT OFTEN SEPARATES THE WINNERS FROM THE LOSERS."

"Self-control in sports often refers to how one reacts to hardships."

"High performance athletes have mastered the art of resiliency."

"RESILIENT THINKERS AREN'T REDUCED BY A LOSS, THEY ARE CHALLENGED BY IT."

"Resilient athletes don't over think, they simply adapt."

"SUCCESS IS NOT JUDGED BY WINNING OR LOSING. IN ATHLETIC COMPETITION, YOU CAN PERFORM ABOVE YOUR CURRENT PEAK LEVEL AND STILL LOSE. YOU CAN ALSO PERFORM WAY BELOW YOUR PERSONAL BEST AND SOMETIMES WIN."

REPETITION

LESSON: The Power of Visual Repetition

A few months back I was a keynote speaker at a USPTA conference, I remember it well because it was freezing cold in early February in Virginia. An ice storm blew in closing Route 76, the I-95 and the airport. Several coaches and I were unlucky enough to be snowed in at the Marriott hotel in Richmond for two days.

In the hotel lobby, I met Roxanne, a charming club pro from Maryland. She and I chatted, passing time as we waited for the storm to lift. Our Starbucks in the lobby switched to lunch in the sports bar as the topic slipped from the typical crazy parent stories to mental training before it turned to visualization. Roxanne and I shared a laugh when she said. "I remember in your seminar you said that imagining success on the court can actually help achieve success. It sounds so... Zen, so Buddha... So, I don't know ...voodoo. Can you explain?"

I mentioned that I've found great success applying visualization to 'dummy up' the over thinkers. Even terrific athletes can get so bogged down by over analyzing their technical components or worrying about not to blowing it that they freeze. "Oh, yes. I've heard it described as paralysis by analysis", she said. "Exactly!" I replied. "Can you walk me through it so I can share it with my clients?" She asked. "I'm buying!" she added.

I began by explaining that we want the athlete to make their critical top patterns and plays automatic subconscious responses. We want the exact correct protocols to be called up when the athlete is so stressed that they can't consciously process in the moment. "When should an athlete rehearse this stuff?" she asked.

The best time to program those subconscious protocols is when the player is falling asleep and again as soon as the player wakes up. This is when the conscious mind isn't quite awake and the subconscious mind is the 'inmate running the asylum'. Not surprisingly, top competitors visualize as part of their pre-game preparation.

Neuroscience studies confirm that visualization actually programs the brain to detect and process clues to aid in anticipating. After imagining their patterns and plays run to perfection, the athlete then responds quicker in real time because they've already seen the 'movie.' When you've seen the movie a thousand times, you anticipate the next scene. Roxanne caught on quickly. "Remember when you spoke about a player's Top 7 Patterns yesterday? So, are you saying that the player imagines themselves running their Top 7 Patterns to perfection and it helps them later to actually run them more efficiently on court?" "You got it!" I said.

I went on to explain additional benefits of visualization. Such as how visualization holds performance goals high above the irrelevant, clutter that intermediate athletes tend to bring into their competition. It's the Law of Attraction. What we think about tends to happen. Visualization helps the player take the appropriate action automatically. This is inviting that automatic 'In the zone' feeling.

"Do you want me to run you through the process?" I asked. "Absolutely!" she responded. I began by explaining that it's quite simple and it's not voodoo or some sort of psychological hypnotizing process.

The process is referred to as Mental Rehearsal. The player gets to a quiet, comfortable, relaxed state. They visualize themselves in a movie. The movie is called "My Greatest Patterns" starring you. The player takes a few minutes to imagine themselves running those elegant swings and shot sequencing patterns to perfection. Their positive visualizations are combined with positive affirmations. The movie is playing each night, every morning and right before practice and competition. It should take ten minutes max. Going up a level isn't always about tweaking the biomechanics of their strokes. It often comes from adding these mental, emotional tools.

"That's terrific! So it's a visual system. I can't wait to get back home to share this with my juniors and my ladies 4.5 league team." Roxanne said.

Visualization is a mental rehearsal, relaxation strategy used to calm performance anxieties and quiet the self-defeating mind.

Mental rehearsal has been applied by top achievers in every field. Visualizing helps analytical thinkers to let go of the conscious and countless details and stressors. This allows their subconscious mind to steer the ship.

"Devise multitasking drills that combine physical, technical, mental and emotional skill sets. Maximizing potential at the quickest rate demands multitasking game components in practice sessions."

"In pre-game preparation, visualizing your top performance patterns keeps your mild full- leaving no room for irrelevant/negative thoughts to intrude."

"Old school coaching methods use repetition to form muscle memory. Unfortunately, muscles don't hold memory. Modern sports science calls muscle memory motor programming."

"Proper motor programming enables an athlete to compete in 'auto pilot' like mode. A motor program involves developing a pathway from the brain to the nervous system and into the muscular system."

RESPONSIBILITY OF ATHLETES

LESSON: **Closing Out a Lead**

Mr. Miguel Rodrigez is an off-road motocross nut. His family lives to breathe the dirt and dust. The more mud that's flying and the louder the motors are screaming, the better. Every weekend he's off to another competition.

He and his three sons Rodney, Randy and Miguel Jr. all compete. They enjoy dirt biking and four wheeling in the California desert. Rodney and Randy are both ranked nationally in the GNCC. Miguel Jr. is only 12 years old, but in dirt biking years he is 7. Seven years of being nurtured by his father and competing daily with his two older brothers has really sped up his learning curve.

While spending time with the Rodrigez boys, I became fascinated by Miguel Jr.'s maturity. He said "I have to compete for everything every day. At meals, if I didn't learn to serve myself, my brothers would take all the food. If I didn't get in the shower early, there would be no hot water. We compete for the TV, the MotoGuy video game, who gets the front seat of the car; there isn't anything we don't compete over. They never let me win. I have to always outsmart them."

It's easy to see why often the youngest sibling becomes the most accomplished member in a sport. They learn from the older siblings failures and they experience the essential traits of competing.

I asked Randy about his competitive experiences and he was very open to discuss his strengths and weaknesses. Randy said he wasn't good at closing out his leads when he first started to compete. "I'd always jump out to a lead then get nervous. The closer I got to the finish line the more I took my hand off the throttle and became safe. My focus somehow shifted from racing to win to racing not to lose. I got so paranoid that I might blow it, that I slowed down and started to ride the brakes. As soon as I realized that I changed my winning style of racing to a scared style of not losing, it was too late. Some fool would pass me and steal first place."

Rodney couldn't resist the rub, "Yea... I can't even count the number of times that Randy blew by me at the start of a race and then let me back in it to win it. I've got a room full of trophies to prove it! Once he learned that racing to win and racing not to lose were two very different mindsets, I was toast. That's why he's ranked above me now."

In most competitions, a common blunder is building a nice comfortable lead by being aggressive then taking your foot off the gas pedal when you see the finish line. At the higher levels of sports, being safe at closing time is actually silly. It is trading a winning strategy in for an unknown strategy. The courage to keep your foot firmly on the gas until you have blown past the finish line is the recipe for success.

"Champions play to win at crunch time. Courage wins titles."

"UNDERSTAND THAT IT'S A PRIVILEGE TO COMPETE. THERE ARE THOUSANDS OF KIDS AS TALENTED AS YOU WHO'LL NEVER GET A SHOT."

"Most children want the glory and the status of being a world class athlete without the countless hours of hard work."

"Take responsibility for your thoughts, your actions and your results."

"After all the parenting and the coaching is said and done, it is up to you to trust your training and execute."

"Seek visible, tangible improvements each week."

"Nothing motivates, inspires and builds confidence like positive results."

"MOST OFTEN WINNERS SPOT THE TIPPING POINTS AND PLAY TO WIN. LOSERS SPOT THEM AND PLAY NOT TO LOSE."

"Champions apply intelligent risks called controlled aggression."

RESPONSIBILITY OF PARENTS

"CHILDREN CAN LEARN THE TECHNICAL NUANCES AND STRATEGIES FROM AN EXPERT COACH AND INCREASED SPEED AND AGILITY FROM A TRAINER, BUT MANAGING THE EMOTIONAL DEVELOPMENT AND LIFE SKILLS WILL COME FROM YOU, THE PARENT."

"Instead of asking your child, 'Did you win?' ask them, 'Did you hit your performance goals?'"

"A PARENTAL RESPONSIBILITY ISN'T TO CONTROL AND LEAD THEIR CHILD FOREVER; IT IS TO ASSIST THEIR CHILD IN DEVELOPING THEIR OWN LEADERSHIP SKILLS."

"Parents your anxieties (worry, stress and fear) are often the cause of your child's performance anxieties."

"UNEDUCATED PARENTS OF ATHLETES WASTE THOUSANDS OF HOURS, DOLLARS, SWEAT AND TEARS."

"HIGH PERFORMANCE ATHLETIC PARENTING IS A FULL-TIME JOB."

"PARENTS SHOULD PROVIDE A SAFE HAVEN FOR HIGH PERFORMANCE ATHLETES TO DEVELOP WITHIN THEIR OWN UNIQUE DEVELOPMENTAL SCHEDULES."

"How can you expect your child to focus on their performance goals when all you ever ask them is: Did you win?"

"NEVER LOSE SIGHT OF THE TRUE BENEFITS OF SPORTS. THEY TEACH WORLD CLASS LIFELONG NAVIGATIONAL SKILLS."

RULES

"Exceptions shadow every rule in life. The trick to high performance athletics is to understand that, most often, the best percentage play is sticking to the rules."

"Warm up rule: Don't show all your weapons, strengths and secrets. Save some for those big moments."

"IN EVERY FIELD, SOMEONE IS WILLING TO STEP OUTSIDE THE BOX (NORM) AND TRY NEW WAYS TO IMPROVE. THAT IS THE EVOLUTION OF SUCCESS."

S

SACRIFICE

"YOU CAN'T BE A NORMAL TEEN AND A CHAMPION. CHAMPIONS ARE BORN OF GREAT SACRIFICE."

"Parents, plan on missing summer activities and most normal holidays. That's when most nationals take place."

"Dedicate yourself by age 11 if you seek world class results."

"AN ASPIRING ATHLETE SHOULD PLAN ON TRAINING THE TECHNICAL, PHYSICAL, MENTAL AND EMOTIONAL COMPONENTS OF THEIR SPORT FOR ABOUT 20 HOURS A WEEK."

"SERIOUS ATHLETES PUT THEIR SPORT AHEAD OF THEIR SOCIAL LIFE."

"You must be willing to sacrifice your old ways in order to become who you want to become."

"SELFISH PARENTS WHO AREN'T WILLING TO SACRIFICE SHOULDN'T EXPECT CHAMPIONSHIP RESULTS IN THEIR CHILDREN."

"You must be willing to sacrifice something good in order to get something great."

"PARENTS, SACRIFICE WINNING THE MEANINGLESS DAILY BATTLES. YOU DON'T ALWAYS HAVE TO BE RIGHT."

SELF-CONTROL

"In high performance sports, one must master the art of controlling the mind, body and emotions."

"In competition, athletes need to trust their training instead of following their reckless impulses and emotions."

"UNDER STRESSFUL CONDITIONS, CALMNESS AND TRUST AT THE CORE SEPARATES WINNERS FROM LOSERS."

"Anger management, mistake management and focus management are self-control components found in rituals and routines."

"Talented athletes with no self-control are nightmares for coaches and are often systematically left out of the lineup."

"DISCIPLINE IS ORGANIZED SELF-CONTROL."

"SELF-CONTROL IS BEING ACCOUNTABLE FOR YOUR THOUGHTS AND ACTIONS."

SELF-DISCIPLINE

LESSON: **The Handicapped Princess**

I met JoAnne Klickstein when I was working with parents, coaches and athletes in Australia. She obviously loved and adored her daughter Elaine. She told me she was willing to help Elaine, in any way to reach her athletic goal.

As we spoke, it became quite clear that JoAnne's words did not match her actions. Though she said she understood that Elaine needed positive and inspirational support to be able to perform confidently under the stress of competition, sadly, JoAnne's parenting style had created anything but a confident belief system for Elaine. Mrs. Klickstein was unknowingly encouraging poor self-reliance/self-discipline, zero accountability or problem solving skills.

After our parental workshop, I was invited to travel with them to a $25K WTA pro challenger event. I was surprised that JoAnne treated Elaine like a handicapped princess. JoAnne everything for Elaine: unpacked her clothes, ordered room service breakfast so Elaine could sleep in longer, packed her equipment bag, carried her bags for her at the event, loaded all of Elaine's suitcases, backpack and tote into the cabs, filled out her tournament documents, fetched ice and towels, spent hours searching the city for her favorite type of filtered bottled water, practice courts, sparring partners, picked up her balls after each practice session...etc. Elaine was 17 years old.

As the event transpired, I wasn't surprised to find that Elaine possessed zero confidence in her own positive self-belief system because she was never invited to nurture those attribute by her loving but controlling mother. Everything was always handed to her on a silver platter. After the first day of competition, Elaine's bath was drawn, her comfy sweats and t-shirt laid out and her dinner ordered. Mrs. K and I ate dinner in the hotel's main restaurant.

I asked "How can a child be self-reliant, have self-discipline and the critical self-belief they desperately need at crunch time if they never have to experience problem solving on their own? Do you realize that you are hindering the exact problem solving behavior that you seek?"

As our dinner was winding down, Mrs. Klickstein recognized that she needed to stop doing everything for her daughter. She agreed that in order for Elaine to thrive as a fully functioning adult, she had to begin to solve her own daily life problems. She said "I'm no longer going to be a cause of handicapping my princess. But... she's still always going to be my princess."

"Poor self-discipline leads to a negative self-image which in turn leads to poor performances."

"DISCIPLINED ATHLETES DON'T FOCUS ON THE TRICKS OF THE TRADE, THEY FOCUS ON THE TRADE."

"SELF-DISCIPLINE COMES IN SIMPLE DAILY CHOICES. ASK YOURSELF IF EACH CHOICE TAKES YOU FURTHER AWAY FROM YOUR GOALS OR PULLS YOU CLOSER TO YOUR GOALS."

"Self-discipline has to be achieved way before you can expect world class results."

"Self-disciplined athletes are terrific team leaders in college."

SELF-ESTEEM

"Without a positive self-image and deep belief in oneself, a gifted athlete will never reach their true potential."

"BELIEVE THAT YOU DESERVE THE SUCCESSFUL RESULTS BECAUSE YOU KNOW YOU'RE WORKING HARDER, LONGER AND SMARTER THAN THE REST OF THE FIELD."

"PARENTS, TO INCREASE SELF-ESTEEM, LIST EVERYTHING YOUR CHILD IS DOING BETTER INSTEAD OF LISTING EVERYTHING YOUR CHILD IS DOING WRONG."

SELFISHNESS

"ATHLETIC ROYALTY IS A DIRECT RESULT OF PARENTAL SACRIFICES."

"Parents cannot have a normal, average life if they are serious about raising athletic royalty."

"EVERY CHAMPION HAS THE RESPONSIBILITY TO GIVE BACK TO THE LESSER KIDS."

"Raising athletic royalty isn't for the selfish parent; it's for the selfless parent. To raise athletic royalty, parents must be prepared to put their own wants and needs aside."

"STRONG PARENTS ARE STRONG BECAUSE THEY'RE ALWAYS LIFTING THEIR JUNIOR ATHLETES UP."

SETBACKS (INJURIES)

LESSON: **Injuries Don't Have to be Setbacks**

Injuries are common issues for every high level athlete. Pushing your body to higher limits means that sports related injuries are expected. Injuries don't always mean that you are doing something wrong. It could actually mean that you are doing things right!

Jenny was a top club level softball player from Anaheim, California. She regularly participated on the First Choice Softball tournament teams. She loved softball and has her heart set on playing NCAA ball at UCLA.

We had been working together for a few years when she and her father called me on speaker phone while driving home from the doctor's office. "Frank, bad news...Jenny just fell in practice and strained her extensor muscle in her right throwing arm. The doctor's orders are no softball training for 6-8 weeks."

Jenny and her father, Jim, share the judger personality profile. Judgers believe that rules and laws should apply to everyone.

That's why they were confused when they heard my reply about the doctor's order with regards to her injury.

I said how sorry I was to hear about Jenny's arm, but that doesn't mean that she should stop training. "What?" Jenny cried out from the passenger seat, "The doctor said no softball!" I said, "Jenny I heard, but just hear me out. This is actually great because there aren't any big tournaments for a few months anyway and we can focus exclusively on your core and lower body strength, speed and agility." Jenny said half-heartedly, "Great."

While most inexperienced parents and athletes would waste two months doing nothing while allowing the arm to mend, Jim agreed that this would be a wonderful opportunity to strengthen other areas of Jenny's game. The three of us met the next day and put into place a brand new developmental plan. We included lower body weight training, spin sessions, yoga flexibility, daily beach runs, incline hill sprints, and a new nutritional plan.

At the end of the eight weeks, Jenny made some serious improvements. She dropped 16 lbs. while adding lean muscle mass. She improved her speed in the 60 ft. distance sprinting from home to first base. She boosted her stamina enough to make her a real threat in those double headers and long weekend tournament play. Most significantly, Jenny's core strength nearly doubled.

Folks that understand sports science know that blocking the third link (core) of the kinetic chain is what catapults the forth link (arms) to accelerate faster than human muscle can contract. A stronger core acts as the blocking link of a human whip. That translates to increased power at the plate.

Injuries don't always mean stop training completely. They simply assist you in switching your child's developmental plan to a different component. Next injury, Jenny wants to tackle her emotional component of her batter's box performance anxiety.

Note: Parents remember that injuries can often lead to greater performance if handled properly. No one improves while doing nothing...mentally, emotionally and/or physically.

"WHEN INJURED, IT DOESN'T MEAN REST. CHAMPIONS KNOW THERE ARE ALWAYS COMPONENTS TO WORK ON."

"Proper fitness and strength training will aid in injury prevention."

"LOSSES COME WHEN AN OPPONENT FINDS YOUR WEAKNESSES BEFORE YOU'VE DECIDED TO FIX THEM."

"Losses usually come after you've taken shortcuts."

"Training half-heartedly and becoming unfit leads to injuries and poor result."

SPEED

"THERE ARE TWO TYPES OF SPEED ATHLETES SHOULD FOCUS ON: FOOT SPEED AND BRAIN SPEED. IF THE BRAIN IS FILLED WITH UNNECESSARY DISTRACTIONS, EVEN THE FASTEST RUNNERS WILL HESITATE, OVER THINK AND APPEAR SLOW."

"Junior athletes have gears they have never used. It's your job as parents to gently push them into their higher gears."

"The sport specific I.Q. of the coach determines the speed at which your child maximizes their potential."

"STAMINA TRAINING MAKES YOU FAST AT THE MOST IMPORTANT TIME, WHICH IS AT THE END OF THE COMPETITION."

"COGNITIVE PROCESSING SPEED IS DIRECTLY RELATED TO ATHLETIC EFFICIENCY. GREAT ATHLETES HAVE THE ABILITY TO RECOGNIZE SOLUTIONS AND QUICKLY PULL THE APPROPRIATE TRIGGERS UNDER DURESS."

SPIRITUALITY

LESSON: **Spirituality Through Sports**

Sports bring a deep sense of community- the type of communal attachment that humans desperately need. It transcends the denominational perspective we were born into because sports don't carry religious divisions. Athletics are universal. They transcend boundaries and borders.

Whether I'm attending an Australian Rugby match along with 100,000 of my closest friends, a Davis Cup Tie with 20,000 flag waving fanatics, a women's college volleyball battle with 1,000 screaming fans, or a high school JV freshman field hockey match with 6 parents and a dog, the communal feeling is the same. Multiple hearts beating as one, dedicated to the performers. We are all invested souls on the same wave length.

Athletics bring drama, risk and danger to our lives, and that's why we love them. There's no hiding as an athlete puts himself or herself on the line. Living through those emotions together is why I am constantly engrossed in the drama of sports. One thing is consistent, whether it's recreational dodge ball, a high performance national gymnastics event or a professional golf tournament, sporting event endings are unknown. The drama continues until it is over. That is why sports are so captivating.

While sports are competitive and confrontational, the spirituality of sports brings people together.

"ONE'S TRUE CHARACTER AND SPIRIT COMES OUT THROUGH SPORTS."

"TRUE HAPPINESS CANNOT BE WON WITH A CHAMPIONSHIP TROPHY. THAT KIND OF DEEP SATISFACTION COMES FROM WORKING TOWARDS YOUR FULL POTENTIAL."

"Most obstacles are created by our fears. Those internal 'lies' stop most of us more often than a superior opponent."

"SPORTS HAVE HEALING POWER. THEY ALLOW US TO SET ALL OUR PROBLEMS ASIDE FOR A FEW HOURS."

"HIGH PERFORMANCE SPORTS OPENS UP THE DOORS TO THE WORLD."

STRENGTH

"Focus on developing a tool belt which exposes your strengths. Then run the same old boring, winning plays over and over again."

"A RECIPE FOR SUCCESS: LOOK TO POSITION YOUR STRENGTHS INTO THEIR WEAKNESSES."

"TRUSTING YOUR STRENGTHS AT CRUNCH TIME LEADS TO SURPASSING YOUR EXPECTATIONS."

SUCCESS

"Success begins in the practice sessions. Please don't expect to win championships if you're not truly training at your full capacity."

"HELP OTHERS SUCCEED AND YOU'LL DISCOVER YOUR PATH TO EVEN MORE SUCCESS."

"Success is defined by doing everything in your power to surpass your expectations."

T

TALENT

"WHAT APPEARS TO BE A NATURAL INBORN TALENT IS USUALLY HARD WORK IN DISGUISE."

"A GOOD COACH AND PARENT DEVELOP THEIR PLAYERS TO REACH THE GOAL THEY SEE. A GREAT COACH AND PARENT DEVELOP THEIR PLAYERS TO REACH GOALS THAT THEY DID NOT EVEN IMAGINE."

"First you must develop your talent. Second, you must entrust yourself to use it – especially in pressure situations."

"Coaches would rather have a less talented player with a great work ethic than a gifted physical athlete with a poor work ethic."

"TALENT COMES IN MANY FORMS. IT'S OFTEN THE HIDDEN MENTAL AND EMOTIONAL SKILL SETS THAT SEPARATE THE WINNERS FROM THE LOSERS."

"TALENT LEFT UN-NURTURED IS THE SAD FATE OF MOST OF OUR CHILDREN."

TEAMWORK

LESSON: **The Superstar That Never Was**

Possibly one of the greatest baseball players ever born into this world was Jonathan Miguel from Punta Cana in the Dominican Republic. Jonathan had the physical size, talent, drive, determination, and work ethic to be a zillionaire in Major League Baseball. His brain type and body type were tailor made for the big leagues. His genetic predisposition was perfect. Unfortunately for him and the rest of the world, his parents weren't willing to sacrifice and do what it took to raise athletic royalty.

Jonathan grew up witnessing less talented boys from his small Caribbean island make it to the big show. Sadly, this superstar never saw the bright lights of a big league baseball stadium. He never played in an official little league game.

Jonathan was born into a family with no interest in sports. His father said dreaming of a career in sports wasn't practical. His mother wasn't any better. Her reoccurring answer to his pleas was always the same. "Jonathan, no one from our family ever made it big at anything. We're just simple people, nothing more." Neither parent shared his dream.

Like most families from his island, they were dirt poor. Jonathan's father drove a cab and worked at the local bakery. Each day his mom baby sat the neighborhood children along with Jonathan and his three sisters. Jonathan now 28 years old drives a cab in Santo Domingo. His car radio is always glued to the local sports channel. He drives the city streets in a dreamlike state imagining what it would have been like to have gotten his shot at baseball. Most nights he can be found parked by one of the dozens of local little league baseball diamonds. He grabs a seat on the bleachers watching the privileged kids, as he waits for the call to his next destination.

Parents, without your commitment to becoming educated in the process, your little superstar doesn't have a chance.

"COACHES AND TRAINERS WILL COME AND GO. THE FAMILY IS A 'LIFELONG' TEAM."

"Maximizing potential requires a close-knit team working towards your child's dream."

"IF THE PARENTS ARE DIVIDED, THEN THE ATHLETE WILL SUFFER."

"In this day and age, an athlete with the desire, but without the parental commitment and support has no chance at becoming athletic royalty."

"Champions have an entourage based on unity, teamwork and collaboration."

"TO GET YOUR CHILD TO SEE FURTHER.... HAVE THEM STAND ON THE SHOULDERS OF A GREAT COACH."

"PARENTS, DON'T SIMPLY TELL YOUR CHILDREN WHAT TO DO...DEMONSTRATE AND INSPIRE THEM WITH YOUR ACTIONS."

"While hiring coaches and trainers look past what they've done and what they know and look deeper into their ability to stimulate your child's passion."

"Great coaches don't try to recreate their past success. They apply the student's unique brain and body type to customize the athlete's personal version of greatness."

TENACITY

"TENACITY IS THAT STUBBORN DETERMINATION THAT CONTINUES TO PULL YOU UP AFTER A SETBACK."

"TENACITY IS MENTAL AND EMOTIONAL ENDURANCE."

"Lack of motivation, persistence and tenacity is more contagious than the flu. Assist your child in avoiding the pretenders who try to pull them down and who say it's not possible."

"IMPOSSIBLE: IS A LIE TOLD BY QUITTERS TO PULL YOU INTO THEIR SAD WORLD."

TIPPING POINTS

"In every sport, you will face tipping points. It's how you respond to them that matters."

"WHAT SEPARATES WINNERS FROM LOSERS IS THE CONFIDENCE TO EXECUTE AND CONVERT IN THOSE TIPPING POINT MOMENTS."

"High performance athletes attack tipping points courageously with pre-scripted plays."

"DON'T LET THE STRESS AND FEAR OF TIPPING POINTS STEAL YOUR GAME."

"Close games are won by small margins. The difference is often a result of staying on script versus going rogue."

U

UNITY

"TOGETHER THROUGH SPORTS, SHARE THE JOURNEY OF MAKING MEMORIES."

"To unite the athlete and entourage, occasionally ask all parties to submit their own assessment/progress report. This will often open up new perspective and delivers new insights."

"ROUTINELY UNITE YOUR ENTOURAGE TO KEEP EVERYONE FOCUSED ON PRIORITIZING THE CHALLENGES."

"Parents, when uniting the entourage, engage with questions and not your opinion."

"Team unity starts with everyone sharing the same moral compass."

"Unite the team with a purpose bigger than your athlete. Inspire and challenge your child's coaches and trainers. By raising their bar, you'll improve the sport. "

"INVOLVE THE ATHLETE IN THE DECISION MAKING. OWNERSHIP COMES FROM THE CHILD BEING SELF-RELIANT."

"Parenting young athletes without a customized navigational system is a lot like traveling the globe without a map."

"PARENTS, YOUR LEGACY WILL BE BASED ON HOW WELL YOU INSPIRED YOUR CHILDREN."

W

WARRIOR

LESSON: **Customized Pre-Game Rituals and Routines**

Most clients attending my workshops have children with unbelievable physical talent. They come from all corners of the world with one common thread: they have failed to achieve the success they are truly capable of attaining. Of course, the question they all want answered is; "Why?"

The answers are varied with the exception of one critical component. The athletes lacked a customized pre-game inflexible set of routines and rituals.

Top performers in every field share a terrific little secret. They have taken the time to develop their customized pre-game relaxation routines and rituals. Morphing a talented athlete into a competitive warrior demands the focused development of pre-match routines.

A player's pre-game preparation demands proper periodization training, practicing in the manner in which they are expected to perform, stretching, nutrition/hydration, and positive visualization. It also requires the parents to commit to ONLY focusing on the words and actions that de-stress the player. A parental pre-game 'de-stressing' preparation strategy should include minimizing the importance of the event and focusing on performance goals and enjoying the moment.

"Great performances begin with great game day routines and rituals."

"Before competition, uneducated athletes don't take the time to get into character. Champs have learned to leave their true feelings, aches & pains at the door as they channel their focus into morphing into an athletic warrior."

"LIFE IS FULL OF COMPETITION. LEARNING THE ART OF MANAGING COMPETITION IS A LIFELONG SKILL FROM THE CRADLE TO THE GRAVE."

"Great competitors aren't meek individuals; they are bold confident risk takers."

"Competitors pay attention to the ebb and flow of the game. They adapt, they problem solve and they stay in the moment."

"QUITTERS SEE HARDSHIPS AS REASONS TO GIVE UP; COMPETITORS SEE HARDSHIPS AS CHALLENGES."

"The love of competition separates the good from the great."

"IF A GREAT COMPETITOR LOSES, THEY USUALLY OVERCOOK VERSUS UNDERCOOK. THEY PLAY TO WIN."

"A satisfied, complacent athlete is headed for a downward spiral. A competitive warrior is always looking to improve."

"GREATNESS IS SIMPLY BEING GOOD AFTER GOOD."

"GREAT COMPETITIVE WARRIORS REALIZE THAT BY PUMPING UP THEIR ADRENALINE THEY ARE INFLATING THEIR ENERGY WHILE DEFLATING THEIR OPPONENT'S ENERGY."

"Champions understand that raising their adrenaline levels at crunch time is the difference between winning and losing."

WEAKNESSES

"In youth sports development, a parental weakness is the inability to compromise. Children need to feel that they are part of the decision making process."

"EVERYONE IS BORN WITH GENETIC STRENGTHS AND WEAKNESSES. IDENTIFY AND CUSTOMIZE YOUR DEVELOPMENTAL PLAN ACCORDINGLY."

"Admitting your weaknesses shows strength in character."

"Recognizing your weaknesses is the first step of improvement."

"It takes courage to improve upon your strengths and attack your limitations."

"IMPROVE YOUR STRENGTHS AND YOUR OPPONENTS WON'T BE ABLE TO FIND YOUR WEAKNESSES."

"THE MOST COMMON WEAKNESS OF HIGH PERFORMANCE PARENTS IS NEGLECTING TO TELL THEIR CHILDREN HOW PROUD THEY ARE TO BE THEIR PARENTS."

WILL (EMOTIONAL EFFORT)

"EMOTIONAL INVESTMENT MAKES THE SEEMINGLY IMPOSSIBLE ... INEVITABLE."

"PARENTS, TEACH YOUR CHILDREN TO HAVE THE COURAGE TO NURTURE THEIR DREAMS OR THEY'LL GROW OLD NURTURING SOMEONE ELSE'S."

"Nothing builds the desire to succeed like success. Position your athlete into winnable opportunities."

"Players who play it safe are trying not to look bad. Players who play to win are trying to look great."

"KIDS OFTEN SAY, 'I'LL TRAIN LIKE A PRO AFTER I TURN PRO.' GREAT REWARDS ONLY COME AFTER YEARS OF GREAT EFFORT."

WINNERS

LESSON: **Winners Are Nurtured Differently**

Parents, let's take a moment and focus on you. One of the most critical parental failures committed while raising athletic royalty is the way in which some parents choose to navigate their world. Kids tend to copy your actions and ignore your wishes. The way you handle situations speaks volumes to your children. Your attitude, thoughts and daily moral code are being imprinted into your child's psyche every hour of every day.

While on a recent trip to Tobago, for an International Tennis Federation event, I had the opportunity to meet two fathers with opposing personality profiles; Mr. Vincent Lorenzo and Mr. Olson White. Both fathers had kids competing in the tournament, they were both in their mid-40's, slightly balding and carrying a few extra pounds. Ironically, they both resided in New Jersey.

Like South Florida, tropical rain fall came like clockwork in Tobago. During the daily rain delays, we spoke for hours on end under the tournament tent. I found that while the sons of Mr. Lorenzo and Mr. White had similar training environments, their inner sanctuary proved to be polar opposites.

Here are my observations after spending three days with the two east coast dads:

Mr Lorenzo fosters trust and belief in people. His New Jersey neighbor, Mr. White rolls his eyes and doubts everything and everyone. Mr. Lorenzo thinks things through, decides on an action plan and acts. Mr. White freezes, hesitates, over thinks about every possible failure and then fails to act in a timely manner. Mr. Lorenzo focuses on the solution to a problem while Mr. White only complains about the same problem for hours and hours on end.

Mr Lorenzo prepares protocols to handle difficult situations beforehand. Mr. White has prepared dozens of excuses. Mr. Lorenzo is fine with working and earning his way through the world. Mr. White wishes and hopes he'll win the lottery. While others talk, Mr. Lorenzo listens and retains pertinent information that may prove meaningful in the future while Mr. White rolls his eyes, believing he already knows it all, and doesn't bother to listen because he is too busy thinking of a way to one-up the others.

Mr. Lorenzo plans and visualizes success and Mr. White obsesses and complains about how nothing ever seems to work out for him.

Now, put yourself in the shoes of a NCAA coach with one full scholarship left to give away. Without ever meeting their boys, would you pick young Tony Lorenzo or young Stanley White?

Top coaches try to interview and spend time with the parents and junior coaches of their prospects to understand what's being nurtured into the athlete. After all, the coach will have to deal with the baggage that comes along with the recruits.

Parents, remember that an experienced coach can teach the technical nuances of a sport. A dedicated trainer can assist in building strong muscles and stamina. But you are your child's life skills master teacher. Pay attention to your attitude, thoughts and actions because great athletes are nurtured differently than good athletes.

"WINNING STEMS FROM CHOOSING THE HARDER CHOICES EVERY DAY."

"Every winner has felt the pain of losing but chooses to battle on."

"SHOW ME A WINNER AND I'LL SHOW YOU A PERSON THAT DOES WHAT OTHERS ARE TOO WEAK TO DO."

"Winners have the faith to jump off a cliff ... and believe they have the skills to figure out how to land on the way down."

"EVERY ATHLETE IS BORN WITH NATURAL EFFICIENCIES. CHAMPIONS ARE BROUGHT TO LIFE BY OVERCOMING THEIR NATURAL DEFICIENCIES."

WORK ETHIC

"SHOW ME AN ATHLETE WHO ALLOWS THEMSELVES TO GIVE HALF EFFORT IN PRACTICE AND I'LL SHOW YOU AN ATHLETE WHO'LL CRACK UNDER THE SLIGHTEST BIT OF GAME DAY PRESSURE."

"Every hobbyist little leaguer wants to go bat during the World Series, every soccer player wants to kick the ball around during World Cup, every football player wants to throw the pigskin during the Super Bowl and every tennis player wants to play a set during Wimbledon. Only the committed want to practice the rest of the year."

"THINK 20% ABOUT THE RANKINGS, THE RIVALS, THE OBSTACLES, THE RESULTS AND 80% ABOUT

ENJOYING THE PROCESS OF IMPROVING AND YOU'LL
BE FAMOUS."

"Full commitment is the only path to athletic royalty."

"FULL UNCONDITIONAL EFFORT IS THE GREATEST
VICTORY (WIN OR LOSE)."

"WITHOUT POSITIVE MOTIVATION AND ENTHUSIASM
THERE IS NO TRUE EFFORT. WITHOUT EFFORT, THERE
IS NO SUCCESS."

"WORK ETHIC TRUMPS PERFECT TECHNIQUE AND
NATURAL TALENT."

*"In practice sessions, average players turn up their
excuses, champions turn up their efforts."*

*"Greatness requires putting your sport above your social
calendar. This applies to both the parents and the
athletes."*

X

X'S & O'S (STRATEGIES / TACTICS)

"The mental toughness component relates to the analytical game decisions. These are the X's & O's of strategy and tactics."

"IF A TACTICAL PLAY WORKS 2 OUT OF 3 TIMES, DO IT RELIGIOUSLY AND YOU'LL WIN THE CONTEST. INEXPERIENCED PLAYERS SWITCH A WINNING TACTIC BECAUSE THEY THINK THAT MAYBE, THE OPPOSITION MAY BEGIN TO FIGURE IT OUT SOMETIME SOON, AND USUALLY END UP LOSING."

"A GREAT STRATEGY IS TO AVOID ALLOWING THE OPPONENTS TO COMFORTABLY APPLY THEIR STRENGTHS."

"Strategy is the overall game plan, the tactics are the applied plays used to maintain the strategic position."

"The X's & O's of successful competition should be based on the high percentage plays not the exceptions to the rules."

"STRATEGY REQUIRES PRE-GAME TACTICAL DEVELOPMENT AS WELL AS GAME TIME OBSERVATION AND OPPONENT PROFILING."

Z

ZONE

LESSON: **Parental Fear, Stress and Overthinking**

Courtney is a future star and USA nationally ranked gymnast. She lives in Bend, Oregon and is home schooled so she can focus on her training. Courtney performs in the zone and religiously nails her routine in practice but seems to falter in actual competition.

Her mom, Kelly, called me and wanted to discuss this disconnect. "How can my daughter be so talented and never win? We do this full time. I leave no stone unturned. Courtney knows the importance of national events. Winning the Nationals is her ticket to the Olympics but she always finds a way to choke. What's wrong with her?"

We set up a Skype session and began to uncover why Courtney was having difficulties in competition. I asked Courtney why she felt that she was not getting the results she was capable of achieving. Quickly, Kelly interrupted, "Her head gets in the way; she's so worried all the time."

I then ask Courtney another conversation opener, "Courtney, performing at your peak potential requires you to begin with your pre-routine relaxation rituals. Can you tell me about yours?" Once again, Kelly jumps into the conversation, "I talk to Courtney to pump her up before each event. She acts like she doesn't want to hear it."

I was beginning to see the stressor that was blocking young Courtney's ability to perform in a relaxed, positive, confident state of mind. Just to be sure, I ask Courtney one more question, "Courtney, have you ever heard of this statement: Focus on controlling the controllables and let go of the uncontrollables?" Once again, Kelly interrupts and adds, "Honey, he means your routine."

Within the first few minutes of our hour long Skype session, their story was already unfolding. Kids aren't born with fear and stress. These are learned behaviors. Kelly is both the reason Courtney is a gymnast and the stressor that is preventing Courtney from performing at her peak performance.

I then told Courtney that I would share a very similar situation I had with another gymnast from California. But first I had two questions for Courtney about an athlete's ability to only focus on the exact protocols needed to perform at their peak- controlling the controllables. (Controllables are the thoughts, attitudes and feelings that pull you closer to your goal of an excellent routine. Uncontrollables are the thoughts that pull you away from focusing solely on your performance routine.)

I asked if Courtney could name a few controllables? Surprisingly, Kelly allowed Courtney to answer and she did brilliantly, "It's, like, my cadence, my breathing, my landings?"

"You nailed it!" I said, Then I asked, "Can you name any uncontrollable thoughts that shouldn't be in your head during competition?"

Courtney replied, "Hum.... I guess … choking?... and…winning the whole event."

"You are correct sister!" I enthusiastically responded.

I followed up with telling her about my familiar story:

A few years ago, I worked with a gal from California with almost the identical difficulties in regards to competing. She and her mom viewed each event as a loss, if she didn't win the whole thing. We talked about flipping her goal from always having to win the event to simply perform an excellent routine. Her best overall score in a national event was 8.6.

So in her next event, the Winter Nationals, she scored an overall 9.4 - exceeding her best score ever! Then an hour later, a competitor nailed her Double Twisting Double Layout and scored an overall 9.5 to take the title.

I then asked Courtney, "Did my gal control her controllables and perform better than she's ever performed in a national?"

"Yes, she exceeded her best score ever, right?" asked Courtney.

"Absolutely, she performed better than ever. She achieved her goal of improving her performance- a very important goal for a competitor your age. Could she control her opponent's performance?"

"No." Courtney said, "That's an uncontrollable, right?" "Right"

For the rest of the Skype session, I chatted with Kelly about her parental role of de-stressing Courtney prior to competition rather than adding stress. We talked about the ability to nurture letting go of the outcome and focus on the performance. Courtney's issues were really manifested by Kelly's worries, stress and fear. Kelly promised to pay attention to her own attitudes and thoughts and try to enjoy the journey instead of agonizing over Courtney's gymnastics.

Parents, if your focus and stress are all about the outcome, how is it possible to expect your child to focus on their performance. After all, isn't that what matters most? Performing in the zone requires trusting your skills and letting go of the uncontrollables.

"Performing in the zone requires trusting intuitive feelings…it feels relaxed, fun and free."

"In the zone, technique, movement and breathing should be thoughtless and effortless."

"In the zone, mental decision making is completed in milliseconds, without any emotional worry, stress or second guessing."

"EATING AND DRINKING ARE GREAT EXAMPLES OF PERFORMING IN THE ZONE. WE DON'T HAVE TO THINK ABOUT THE MOTOR PROGRAMS REQUIRED IN LIFTING THE GLASS TO THE MOUTH OR CONSCIOUSLY PROCESS THE CHEWING OF OUR FOOD. PERFORMING TASKS EFFORTLESSLY IN SPORTS REQUIRES THE SAME TRUST WITHOUT FEAR."

"The surest way to kill playing in the zone is to try and figure out how and why you are in the zone. To stay in the zone, stop overthinking and simply enjoy the flow."

"APPLYING MENTAL REHEARSALS IS PRE-PLANNING THE EXACT MOTOR PROGRAMS AND SOLUTION PROTOCOLS WHICH INVITES THE 'ZONE' LIKE PERFORMANCES. IMAGINING EACH COMPONENT BEING PERFORMED CORRECTLY PRE-SETS SUCCESS."

"PERFORMING IN THE ZONE REQUIRES LESS THINKING ABOUT TECHNIQUE, MOVEMENT, STRATEGIES AND RESULTS."

CONCLUSION

There is no doubt that parental modeling plays the most significant role in the way an athlete is nurtured. Children instinctively imitate their parent's behaviors, attitudes and moral conduct.

The code of excellence we all wish to imprint on our children cannot be taught in only a few hours a week by a gifted coach. These life lessons need to be nurtured day in and day out by their parents.

The true benefit of this book lies not solely in the scripts, quotes and lessons, but in the actions they inspire. Please remember, your child was born pre-wired with a set of specific skills and preferences. Combining their genetic predisposition, a deliberate customized navigational blueprint and *Raising Athletic Royalty's* insights will result in what scientists call a combination of emergent properties:

A perfect storm of your child's genetic predispositions, proper nurturing and customized training equals Athletic Royalty.

Best of luck as you begin to instill powerful life lessons and develop positive, self-confident, self-sufficient young adults.

Enjoy your new journey of *Raising Athletic Royalty*.

Frank

ABOUT THE AUTHOR

Frank Giampaolo is a 30 year sports education veteran. He was honored as the USPTA Southern California Tennis Director of the Year and received numerous awards as a top teaching professional by Southern California Tennis & Golf Magazine.

Frank is a popular convention speaker, a sports educator, instructional writer for ITF (International Tennis Federation) Coaching & Sports Science Review, UK Tennis magazine, the USPTA, Tennis Magazine and Tennis View Magazine. He is an author of *Championship Tennis* (Human Kinetics Publishing), *The Tennis Parent's Bible*, The Mental Emotional Workbook Series (*How to Attract a College Scholarship, International Player Evaluation, Match Chart Collection, Match Day Preparation and Blunders* and *Cures*). His television appearances include The NBC Today Show, OCN-World Team Tennis, Fox Sports, Tennis Canada and Tennis Australia.

Frank founded The Tennis Parents Workshops in 1998, conducting workshops across the United States, Mexico, Israel, New Zealand, Australia, Canada and Spain. He then instituted The Mental/Emotional Tennis Workshops in the spring of 2002. Frank's commitment to coaching excellence helped develop 77 National Champions, hundreds of NCAA athletes, numerous NCAA All-Americans and several professional athletes. His innovative approach has made him a worldwide leader in athletic-parental education. Frank is currently the Vice Chair of the USTA/SCTA Coaches Commission.

Contact Information

Email: FGSA@earthlink.net

Website: www.RaisingAthleticRoyalty.com

Website: www.MaximizingTennisPotential.com

Facebook:
http://facebook.com/FrankGiampaoloBooks.The Tennis Parent Bible

Google:
http://plus.google.com/u/0/+FrankGiampaolo/posts

Twitter: http://twitter.com/@Frank_Giampaolo

Made in the USA
San Bernardino, CA
06 March 2019